SARAH DALLAS **KNITTING**

SARAH DALLAS **KNITTING**

PHOTOGRAPHS **CATHERINE GRATWICKE**

Martingale®
& COMPANY

To Georgie

Martingale®
& C O M P A N Y

Martingale & Company
20205 144th Avenue NE
Woodinville, WA 98072-8478, USA
www.martingale-pub.com

First published in 2005 by Rowan Yarns
Holmfirth, West Yorkshire, HD9 2DX, UK
Copyright © Rowan Yarns 2005

First published in the USA by Martingale & Company

Design & art direction **Georgina Rhodes**
& **Richard Proctor**
Stylist **Francine Kay**
Editor **Sally Harding**
Pattern writer **Eva Yates**
Pattern checker **Stella Smith**

Cataloging in Publication Data is available
10 09 08 07 06 05 8 7 6 5 4 3 2 1
ISBN 1-56477-637-9
Printed in Singapore

Contents

Introduction

This book was inspired by a family vacation in Dorset several years ago, which reminded me of vacations I spent as a child playing on the beach and then wrapping up to go home at the end of the day. The changeable weather during a typical seaside summer vacation means being prepared for all eventualities: clothes to enjoy the afternoon sun, to protect you against the wind, and to keep you warm and comfortable on cool evenings. As a result, my designs for this book include sweaters, cardigans, jackets, socks, blankets, cushions, and even a camisole. All of them are functional pieces: cushions and blankets to throw down on the beach for a picnic (and for warmth at home in the evening), socks to wear indoors or out, and cardigans and jackets for comfort and style. The mood of the book, perhaps subconsciously, reflects my own lifestyle; living in London yet craving the calmer comforts of life in the country, memories of childhood, playing with friends outside, rambling across the fields or along the beach, collecting leaves, flowers, and pebbles. As a result, the designs combine the feeling of modern, urban living with traditional crafts; of contrasts coming together.

Color is one of the most important elements for me in the design process.

The changing colors of the seasons are particularly inspiring: the crisp, sharp flushes of spring; the intense, vivid hues of summer; the rich, warm glows of fall; and the dark, somber shades of winter. The combinations, the proportions, and the balance of colors, whether in large blocks, stripes, Fair Isles, or the fine detail of a color-tipped edge of a blanket, cushion, or cardigan, are all critical.

Flowers are a constant source of inspiration for color and provide the spectrum of colors chosen for the book. These include the clean, fresh colors of tulips, lilac, cornflowers, and lavender and the bright, vibrant hues of poppies, peonies, roses, gerberas, and ranunculus. Seen against the blacks and grays of the urban environment, these contrasting groupings of color eventually work together to provide the overall palette.

Shape and silhouette are also crucial to the design of any garment or accessory as is the type and quality of yarns used; crisp cottons, soft wools, nubby tweeds, and slubby silks, and never more importantly so than when the pieces have a simplicity to them for a modern, contemporary lifestyle. The final outcome of all these elements is a collection of easy, functional pieces to knit for the family, the home, the garden, and the beach.

Sarah Dallas
London, January 2005

LAVENDER/ROSE

Late summer and early fall have
a richness in the color palette that
never fails to inspire me. From the last
flush of brilliant flowers against a
golden sky to the cozy warmth of
evenings as they draw in, there is a
magical element to the closing days of
summer. Colder evenings ask for warm
socks, afghans to cuddle up in, or a
cardigan to slip over a summer dress.
Lavender, rose, crimson, and lime
combine in unexpected ways to give
quite simple designs an unusual twist.

Cotton Cardigan
In vibrant pink medium-weight cotton yarn, this cardigan with its neat ribbed collar and pocket details is the ideal cover-up for cooler evenings. Simple to knit, it has garter-stitch rib panels on the front and sleeves. Page 22.

Stripy Socks

Ideal for walking around the house on cool mornings or evenings, these crimson and fuchsia pink striped socks are knitted in cozy merino wool. With the toes and heels picked out in red, and with a contrasting-colored tip on the ribbing, they look as good as they feel. Page 24.

Fair Isle Socks

With their simplified Fair Isle border, these socks are knitted in the same yarn as the stripy pair. Page 25.

Gloves

These gloves are also knitted in the same yarn as the socks, and are similarly tipped with a contrasting color on the ribbing. Page 26.

Rothko-style Afghan
Inspired by Mark
Rothko's bold abstract
paintings, this afghan
could not be simpler.
Knitted in three strong
colors, with fine
contrasting borders, it
creates a marvelous
splash of brilliant color.
Page 28.

Rothko-style Pillow
The pillow is designed
to coordinate with the
afghan (left),
incorporating the
same vivid blocks of
color divided by the
sharpness of the green.
Page 29.

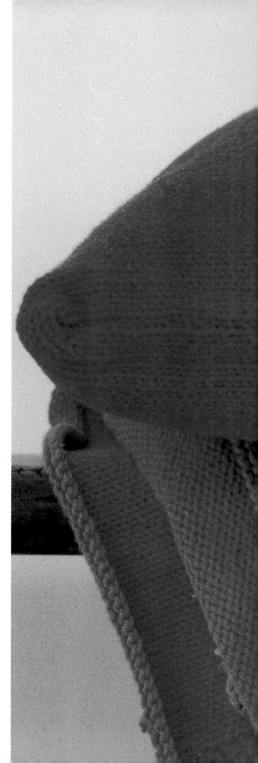

Beret

In flattering lavender
merino wool, this classic
beret suits everyone.
The contrasting tip on
the ribbing provides just
the right touch of color.
Page 30.

Three-textured Afghan

Knitted in crisp cotton yarn, in blocks of three different garter-stitch patterns, this textured afghan has been created in shades of lilac and pink, offset by details of contrasting greenish tones.

Page 31.

Cotton Cardigan

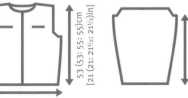

46 (49: 52: 55)cm
[18 (19½: 20½: 21½)in]

53 (53: 55: 55)cm
[21 (21: 21½: 21½)in]

44cm [17½ in]

SIZES & YARN

Size	S	M	L	XL	
To fit bust	34	36	38	40	in
	86	91	96	102	cm
Actual size	36	38½	41	43½	in
	92	98	104	110	cm
Length to shoulder	20	20	21	21	in
	51	51	53	53	cm
Sleeve length	17½	17½	17½	17½	in
	44	44	44	44	cm

Rowan Handknit DK Cotton, 50g balls

Pink (313)	13	14	15	16

9 buttons

NEEDLES

1 pair each of size 3 (3.25mm) and size 6 (4mm) needles. Stitch holder.

GAUGE

20 sts and 28 rows to 4in (10cm) measured over St st using size 6 (4mm) needles.

BACK

Using size 3 (3.25mm) needles, cast on 86 (90: 98: 102) sts. Work in garter rib as folls:

Row 1 *K2, P2, rep from * to last 2 sts, K2.
Row 2 P to end.
Rows 3 to 14 Rep rows 1 and 2 six times. Sizes 2 and 4 ONLY, inc 1 st at each end of last row. Change to size 6 (4mm) needles and St st, inc 1 st at each end of 13th and every foll 16th row to 92 (98: 104: 110) sts. Cont without shaping until work meas 12½ (12½: 13: 13)in [32 (32: 33: 33)cm], ending with RS facing for next row.
Shape armholes
Rows 1 and 2 Bind off 2 (3: 4: 4) sts, work to end.
Row 3 K2, ssk, knit to last 4 sts, K2tog, K2.
Row 4 P to end.
Rep rows 3 and 4 until 78 (82: 84: 88) sts rem. Cont without shaping until work meas 20 (20: 21: 21)in [51 (51: 53: 53)cm], ending with RS facing for next row.
Shape shoulders
Bind off 5 (5: 6: 6) sts at beg of next 6 rows.
Bind off 6 (7: 5: 6) sts beg next 2 rows. Bind off.

POCKETS (make 2)

Using size 6 (4mm) needles, cast on 18 sts and work 28 rows in St st. Leave sts on holder.

LEFT FRONT

Using size 3 (3.25mm) needles, cast on 42 (44: 48: 50) sts and work 14 rows in garter rib as folls:

Row 1 *K2, P2, rep from * to last 2 (0: 0: 2) sts, K2 (0: 0: 2).
Row 2 P to end.
Rows 3 to 14 Rep rows 1 and 2 six times. Sizes 2 and 4 ONLY, inc 1 st at end of last row. Change to size 6 (4mm) needles and work as folls:
Row 1 K14 (19: 18: 23), *P2, K2, rep from * three times, P2, K10 (8: 12: 10).
Row 2 P to end.
Rows 1 and 2 form St st with garter rib panel patt. Cont in patt, inc 1 st at beg of 11th and every foll 16th row to 45 (48: 51: 54) sts. Cont without shaping until work meas 12½ (12½: 13: 13)in [32 (32: 33: 33)cm], ending with RS facing for next row.
Shape armhole
Row 1 (RS) Bind off 2 (3: 4: 4) sts, patt to end.
Row 2 P to end.
Row 3 K2, ssk, patt to end.
Row 4 P to end.

Rows 5 to 10 Rep rows 3 and 4 three times. 39 (41: 43: 46) sts.

Row 11 K2, ssk, K7 (11: 9: 14), *P2, K2, rep from *, bind off 2 sts [for pocket buttonhole], *K2, P2, rep from *, K10 (8: 12: 10).

Row 12 P18 (16: 20: 18), cast on 2 sts, P to end.

Rows 13 (K2, ssk) 0(0: 1: 1) times, patt to end.

Row 14 P to end.

Row 15 (K2, sl1, K1, psso) 0 (0: 0: 1) times, patt to end.

Row 16 P10 (8: 12: 10), bind off 18 sts [for top of pocket], P to end.

Row 17 K10 (14: 11: 15), K across pocket sts from holder, K to end. 38 (40: 41: 43) sts.

Row 18 P to end.

Cont in St st, without shaping, until work meas 19 (19: 20: 20)in [48.5 (48.5: 50.5: 50.5)cm], ending with WS facing for next row.

Shape neck

Bind off 8 (9: 9: 10) sts, knit to end. Dec 1 st at neck edge on next 6 rows.

Shape shoulders

Row 1 Bind off 5 (5: 6: 6) sts, K to last 2 sts, K2tog.

Row 2 P to end.

Rows 3 to 6 Rep rows 1 and 2 twice. Bind off.

RIGHT FRONT

Using size 3 (3.25mm) needles, cast on 42 (44: 48: 50) sts and work 14 rows in garter rib as folls:

Row 1 K2 (0: 0: 2), *P2, K2, rep from * to end.

Row 2 P to end.

Rows 3 to 14 Rep rows 1 and 2 six times. Sizes 2 and 4 ONLY, inc 1 st at beg of last row.

Change to size 6 (4mm) needles. Cont as folls:

Row 1 K10 (8: 12: 10), *P2, K2, rep from * 3 times, P2, K to end.

Row 2 P to end.

This sets patt panel. Work to match left front, reversing all shaping.

SLEEVES (make 2)

Using size 3 (3.25mm) needles, cast on 46 (48: 50: 52) sts.

Row 1 (set up row) K0 (1: 2: 3), *P2, K2, rep from * to last 2 (3: 0: 1) sts, P2 (2: 0: 0), K0 (1: 0: 1). Work 13 more rows in garter rib.

Change to size 6 (4mm) needles. Cont as folls:

Row 1 K16 (17: 18: 19) *P2, K2, rep from * twice, P2, K16 (17: 18: 19).

Row 2 P to end.

These two rows form patt panel. Cont in patt, making fully fashioned incs as folls: K2, inc, patt to last 4 sts, inc, K3, on next and every foll 8th row to 74 (76: 78: 80) sts. Cont without shaping until work meas 17½in (44cm).

Shape sleeve cap

Bind off 2 (3: 4: 4) sts at beg of next 2 rows.

Row 3 K2, ssk, patt to last 4 sts, K2tog, K2.

Row 4 P to end.

Rep rows 3 and 4 until 46 sts rem.

Dec 1 st at each end of next 4 rows. Bind off 3 sts at beg of next 4 rows. Bind off.

BUTTON BAND (Left front)

Using size 3 (3.25mm) needles, cast on 7 sts and work in K1, P1 rib until band, when slightly stretched, fits front from hem to neck. Bind off. Sew in place. Mark positions for 7 buttonholes, the first 2 rows above the cast-on edge; the 2nd at top of garter rib; the 7th, ½in (1cm) below the neck; and the rem 4 evenly spaced between (approx 3in [8cm] apart).

BUTTONHOLE BAND (Right front)

Using size 3 (3.25mm) needles, cast on 7 sts. Working in K1, P1 rib, make buttonholes to match marked positions as folls:

Row 1 Rib 3, bind off 2 sts, rib to end.

Row 2 Rib 2, cast on 2 sts, rib to end.

Work to match button band length. Bind off. Sew in place.

COLLAR

Using size 6 (4mm) needles, cast on 90 (90: 94: 98) sts and work as folls:

Row 1 *P2, K2, rep from * to last 2 sts, P2.

Row 2 P to end.

Rep rows 1 and 2 until work measures 3in (8cm), ending with row 1.

Next row P2 (2: 4: 6), *P2tog, P4, rep from * to last 4 (4: 6: 8) sts, P2tog, P2 (2: 4: 6). Bind off.

FINISHING

Block pieces to measurements. Slip stitch pockets in position. Sew shoulder seams. Ease sleeve cap into armhole and sew in place. Sew side and sleeve seams. Place RS of collar to WS of garment, bound-off collar edge to neck, starting and finishing halfway across front bands. Sew in place. Sew buttons on button band and on fronts to match buttonholes on pockets. Weave in loose ends.

Stripy Socks

SIZES & YARNS

To fit	S-M	M-L	
Foot length	9	10	in
	24	26	cm

Rowan 4ply Soft, 50g balls

A Pink (377)	2	2
B Red (374)	1	1
C Light olive (379)	1	1

NEEDLES

4 x size 3 (3mm) double-pointed needles.
4 x size 5 (3.75mm) double-pointed needles.
Spare needle.

GAUGE

26 sts and 32 rows to 4in (10cm) measured over St st using size 5 (3.75mm) needles.

SOCKS

Using size 3 (3mm) needles and yarn C, cast on 66 sts (22 sts on each of 3 needles). Break yarn C, join in yarn B and work 1in (2.5cm) in K1, P1 rib.

Change to size 5 (3.75mm) needles, join in yarn A and work as folls:

Rounds 1 to 6 Using yarn A, K to end.
Round 7 Using yarn B, K2, K2tog, K to last 4 sts, sl1, K1, psso, K2.
Round 8 Using yarn B, K to end.
Rounds 1 to 8 form stripe patt.
Rep rounds 1 to 8 until 52 sts rem. Cont in stripe patt without shaping until work meas approx 10in (26cm), ending on round 6. Break yarns.
Divide sts for heel Slip first 13 sts (on needle 1) and last 13 sts (on needle 3) onto spare needle. Arrange rem sts on 2 needles for instep. Rejoin yarn B and work 20 rows in St st on heel sts, ending with RS facing for next row.
Row 21 K17, K2tog tbl, turn.
Row 22 Sl1, P8, P2tog, turn.
Row 23 Sl1, K8, K2tog tbl, turn.
Rep rows 22 and 23 until 10 sts rem.
Next row Needle 1: K10, pick up 10 sts from side of heel, K1 instep st; needle 2: K24 instep sts; needle 3: K1 instep st, pick up 10 sts from side of heel, K first 5 sts from needle 1. This is new beg of round. (16:24:16 sts).
Shape gusset
Round 1 Needle 1: K to last 3 sts, K2 tog, K1; needle 2: Knit; needle 3: K1, ssk, K to end.

Round 2 Knit around.
Rep these two rounds 2 times more. 50 sts.
Work 1 round even.
Cont stripes.
*Knit 2 rounds yarn B, 6 rounds yarn A, rep from * until foot measures 8 (8½)in [20 (22)cm]. Break yarn A.
Shape toe
Using yarn B, work as folls:
Round 1 Knit around.
Round 2 Needle 1: K to last 3 sts, K2tog, K1; needle 2: K1, ssk, K to last 3 sts, K2tog, K1; needle 3: K1, ssk, K to end.
Cont to dec every alt round until 26 sts rem.
Work one round even.
Turn sock inside-out and slip sts from needle 3 to needle 1. Close toe with 3-needle bind-off.
Make second sock to match.

FINISHING

Weave in loose ends. To block socks, hand wash, roll in a towel to squeeze out excess water, then reshape and spread flat on a towel to dry.

Fair Isle Socks

SIZES & YARNS

To fit	S-M	M-L	
Foot length	9	10	in
	24	26	cm

Rowan 4ply Soft, 50g balls

A Light purple (375)	2	2
B Pink (377)	1	1
C Light olive (379)	1	1
D Pale blue (370)	1	1

NEEDLES

4 x size 2 (3mm) double-pointed needles.
4 x size 3 (3.25mm) double-pointed needles.
4 x size 4 (3.5mm) double-pointed needles.
Spare needle.

GAUGE

28 sts and 36 rows to 4in (10cm) measured over St st using size 3 (3.25mm) needles.

SOCKS

Using size 2 (3mm) needles and yarn C, cast on 64 sts (21: 21: 22 sts). Join in yarn B and work 10 rounds in K1, P1 rib.
Change to size 4 (3.5mm) needles and work

Fair Isle in St st (every round, knit), joining in yarns A and D, as folls.
Round 1 D.
Round 2 *2D, 3A, 3D, 2A, 3D, 2A, 1D, rep from * to end.
Round 3 *1D, 5A, 3D, 2A, 1D, 2A, 2D, rep from * to end.
Round 4 *2B, 3C, 3B, 3C, 1B, 3C, 1B, rep from * to end.
Round 5 Rep round 3.
Round 6 Rep round 2.
Round 7 Rep round 1.
Break yarns C and D.
Change to size 3 (3.25mm) needles and work stripe patt as folls:
Rounds 1 and 2 B.
Rounds 3 to 8 A.
Rep rounds 1 to 8 three times.
Decrease round K2, K2tog, K to last 4 sts, sl1, K1, psso, K2.
Cont in stripe pattern, dec as set on every foll 5th round until 48 sts rem.
Cont without shaping until work meas approx 13in (33cm), ending on round 8.
Break yarns.
Divide sts for heel Slip first 12 sts (on needle

1) and last 12 sts (on needle 3) onto spare needle. Arrange rem sts on 2 needles for instep. Rejoin yarn B and work 20 rows in St st on heel sts.
Row 21 K16, K2tog tbl, turn.
Row 22 Sl1, P8, P2tog, turn.
Row 23 Sl1, K8, K2tog tbl, turn.
Rep rows 22 and 23 until 10 sts rem.
Next row Needle 1: K10, pick up 10 sts from side of heel, K1 instep st; needle 2: K22 instep sts; needle 3: K1 instep st, pick up 10 sts from side of heel, K first 5 sts from needle 1. This is new beg of round. (16:22:16) sts.
Shape gusset
Round 1 Needle 1: K to last 3 sts, K2tog, K1; needle 2: Knit; needle 3: K1, ssk, K to end.
Round 2 Knit around.
Rep these two rounds 2 times more. 48 sts.
Work 1 round even.
*Knit 2 rounds yarn B, 6 rounds yarn A, rep from * until foot measures 8 (8½)in [20 (22)cm].
Break yarn A.
Shape toe
Using yarn B, work as folls:
Round 1 Knit around.

Round 2 Needle 1: K to last 3 sts, K2tog, K1; needle 2: K1, ssk, K to last 3 sts, K2tog, K1; needle 3: K1, ssk, K to end.
Cont to dec every alt round until 24 sts rem. Work one round even.
Turn sock inside out and slip sts from needle 3 to needle 1. Close toe with 3-needle bind off.

FINISHING

Weave in loose ends. To block the socks, hand wash, roll in a towel to squeeze out excess water, then reshape and spread flat on a towel to dry.

Gloves

SIZES & YARNS

Size	S-M	M-L

Rowan 4ply Soft, 50g balls

A Pink (377)	2	2
B Light olive (379)	Small amount for edging.	
C Light purple (375)	Small amount for edging.	

NEEDLES

4 x size 2 (2.75mm) double-pointed needles.
Spare needles.
Safety pin.

GAUGE

32 sts and 40 rows to 4in (10cm) measured over St st using size 2 (2.75mm) needles.

RIGHT GLOVE

Using size 2 (2.75mm) needles and yarn B, cast on 60 sts (20 sts on each of 3 needles). Break yarn B.
Join in yarn A and work 2½in (6cm) in rounds of K1, P1 rib. Change to St st (every round, knit) and work 2 rounds.

Shape thumb gusset

Round 3 K30, inc, K2, inc, K to end.

Knit 3 rounds.
Round 7 K30, inc, K4, inc, K to end.
Knit 3 rounds.
Round 11 K30, inc, K6, inc, K to end.
Cont inc as set to completion of round 23.
72 sts.
Knit 2 rounds.
Round 26 K29, place next 18 sts on safety pin for thumb, cast on 6 sts, complete the round.
60 sts.
Work 20 rounds.
Divide for fingers Slip first 22 sts of round onto spare needle and rejoin yarn A with RS facing.

First finger

**K18 as folls: using spare needle 1, K6, using spare needle 2, K10, turn, cast on 2 sts, turn. Divide the 18 sts on spare needle on 3 needles and knit 24 (30) rounds.

Shape top

Round 1 (K2tog) 9 times.
Round 2 K to end.
Round 3 *K1, K2tog, rep from * to end.
Break yarn, leaving an end to run through the sts, pull tightly, and fasten off.

Second finger

RS facing, rejoin yarn A and K8, cast on 2 sts,

knit the last 8 sts of the rem sts, then pick up and knit 2 sts from the base of the first finger. Divide these 20 sts on 3 needles and knit 28 (34) rounds.

Shape top

Round 1 *K2tog, rep from * to end.
Round 2 K to end.
Round 3 *K2tog, rep from * to end.
Break yarn, leaving an end to run through the sts, pull tightly, and fasten off.

Third finger

RS facing, rejoin yarn A and K7, cast on 2 sts, knit the last 7 sts of the rem sts, then pick up and knit 2 sts from the base of the second finger. Divide these 18 sts on 3 needles and knit 24 (30) rounds.
Shape top as first finger.

Fourth finger

RS facing, rejoin yarn A and K14 and pick up and knit 2 sts from the base of the third finger. Divide these 16 sts on 3 needles and knit 20 (26) rounds.

Shape top

Round 1 *K2tog, rep from * to end.
Round 2 K to end.
Round 3 *K2tog , K1, rep from *, K2tog.

Break yarn, leaving an end to run through the sts, pull tightly, and fasten off.

Thumb

RS facing, rejoin yarn A and K18 from safety pin and pick up and knit 6 sts from base of thumb. Divide these 24 sts on 3 needles and work 20 (24) rounds.

Shape top

Round 1 *K2tog, rep from * to end.

Round 2 K to end.

Round 3 *K2tog, rep from * to end.

Break yarn, leaving an end to run through the sts, pull tightly, and fasten off.**

LEFT GLOVE

Using size 2 (2.75mm) needles and yarn C, cast on 60 sts. Break yarn C. Join in yarn A and work cuff as for right glove. Change to St st and work 2 rounds.

Thumb gusset

Round 3 K26, inc, K2, inc, K to end.

Cont as for right glove with thumb gusset in new position.

Round 26 K25, place next 18 sts on safety pin, cast on 6 sts, K to end.

Work 20 rounds.

Divide for fingers Slip first 20 sts of round onto spare needle and rejoin yarn A with RS facing.

First finger

Work from ** to ** as on right glove.

FINISHING

Weave in any loose ends. To block, hand wash, roll in a towel to squeeze out excess water, then reshape and spread flat to dry.

Rothko-style Afghan

SIZE & YARNS

| Size | 47 x 64in |
| | 120 x 162cm |

Rowan Handknit DK Cotton, 50g balls

A Olive green (219)	3
B Red (215)	1
C Pink (313)	3
D Orange (254)	1

NEEDLES

Size 7 (4.5mm) circular needle at least 24in (61cm) long
Size G/6 (4mm) crochet hook.

GAUGE

19 sts and 26 rows to 4in (10cm) measured over St st using size 7 (4.5mm) needle.

STRIP 1

Using size 7 (4.5mm) needle and yarn A, cast on 114 sts, using long-tail method. Break yarn A, join in yarn B and work as folls:
Row 1 K to end.
Row 2 P to last 5 sts, K5.
These 2 rows form St st with garter-st edge.

Rep rows 1 and 2 until work meas 64in (162cm), ending with row 1. Break yarn B.
Join in yarn C and purl 1 row. Bind off.

STRIP 2

Using size 7 (4.5mm) needle and yarn A, cast on 114 sts, using long-tail method. Break yarn A. Join in yarn C and work as folls:
Row 1 K to end.
Row 2 K5, P to end.
These 2 rows form St st with garter-st edge.
Rep rows 1 and 2 until work meas 44in (112cm), ending with row 2. Break yarn C.
Join in yarn A and knit 2 rows. Break yarn A.
Join in yarn D and rep rows 1 and 2 until work meas 64in (162cm), ending with row 1. Break yarn D.
Join in yarn C and purl 1 row. Bind off.

FINISHING

Block pieces to measurements. With WS together (crochet is on RS as a contrast detail) and using size G/6 (4mm) crochet hook and yarn C, join strips with a row of single crochet to make a decorative seam. Weave in ends.

Rothko-style Pillow

SIZE & YARNS

Size	18 x 18in
	46 x 46cm

Rowan Handknit DK Cotton, 50g balls

A Red (215)	3
B Orange (254)	1
C Pink (313)	3
D Olive green (219)	1

18 x 18in (46 x 46cm) pillow form.

NEEDLES

1 pair each of size 5 (3.75mm) and size 6
(4mm) needles.
4 stitch markers

GAUGE

20 sts and 28 rows to 4in (10cm) measured
over St st using size 6 (4mm) needles.

PILLOW COVER

Using size 5 (3.75mm) needles and yarn B,
cast on 91 sts. Break yarn B. Join in yarn D and
work 6 rows in K1, P1 rib. Break yarn D.
Join in yarn A and change to size 6 (4mm)
needles and St st. Cont until work meas 12in
(30cm). Place markers at each end of last row.
Cont in St st until work meas 18in (46cm),
ending with RS facing for next row.
Break yarn A.
Join in yarn D and knit 2 rows. Break yarn D.
Join in yarn B and change to St st. Cont until
work meas 24in (61cm), ending with RS facing
for next row. Break yarn B.
Join in yarn D and knit 2 rows. Break yarn D.
Join in yarn C and change to St st. Cont until
work meas 30in (76cm). Place markers at each
end of last row. Cont in St st until work meas
39in (99cm), ending with RS facing for next
row. Break yarn C.
Change to size 5 (3.75mm) needles, join in
yarn D and knit 1 row. Change to K1, P1 rib and
work 5 rows. Break yarn D.
Join in yarn B and bind off.

FINISHING

Block to measurements. Place RS together,
fold two ends to the center, using markers as
top and bottom of pillow cover, and
overlapping center back of pillow cover by 4in
(10cm). Sew side seams. Turn RS out. Insert
pillow form.

Beret

SIZE & YARNS

Size

To fit average head   22in circumference.

                             56cm circumference.

Rowan 4ply Soft, 50g balls

A Lavender (375)	1 x 50g
B Red (374)	Small amount for edging.

NEEDLES

1 pair each of size 2 (2.75mm) and size 3
(3.25mm) needles.

GAUGE

28 sts and 36 rows to 4in (10cm) measured
over St st using size 3 (3.25mm) needles.

BERET

Using size 2 (2.75mm) needles and yarn B,
cast on 144 sts. Break yarn B. Join in yarn A
and work 10 rows in K1, P1 rib.
Change to size 3 (3.25mm) needles and St st.
Work as folls:
Increase row *Inc, K1, rep from * to end. 216 sts.
Work 27 rows.

Row 29 *K2tog, K4, rep from * to end. 180 sts.
Work 9 rows.
Row 39 *K2tog, K3, rep from * to end. 144 sts.
Work 7 rows.
Row 47 *K2tog, K2, rep from * to end. 108 sts.
Work 5 rows.
Row 53 *K2tog, K1, rep from * to end. 72 sts.
Work 3 rows.
Row 57 *K2tog, K4, rep from * to end. 60 sts.
Work 1 row.
Row 59 *K2tog, K3, rep from * to end. 48 sts.
Work 1 row.
Row 61 *K2tog, K2, rep from * to end. 36 sts.
Work 1 row.
Row 63 *K2tog, K1, rep from * to end. 24 sts.
Row 64 P2tog across row. 12 sts.
Break yarn, leaving thread for sewing. Thread
yarn through rem sts, pull tightly, and secure.
Weave in any loose ends.

FINISHING

Sew seam. Weave in loose ends. To block,
hand wash, roll in a towel to squeeze out
excess water, then reshape, placing beret over
a dinner plate to dry.

Three-textured Afghan

SIZE & YARNS

Size	48 x 58in
	122 x 147cm

Rowan Cotton Glace, 50g balls

A Light purple (787)	10
B Rose pink (747)	7
C Lilac (811)	4
D Olive green (814)	Small amount for edging.
E Pale lime (813)	Small amount for edging.

NEEDLES

Size 5 (3.75mm) circular needle at least 24in (61cm) long.
Size F/5 (3.75mm) crochet hook.

GAUGE

23 sts and 32 rows to 4in (10cm) measured over block patt using size 5 (3.75mm) needle.

STRIP 1

Using size 5 (3.75mm) needles and yarn D, cast on 140 sts using long-tail method. Break yarn D, join in yarn A and knit 1 row.

Change to block patt and work as folls:
Row 1 *K5, P5, rep from * to last 10 sts, K10.
Row 2 *K5, P5, rep from * to end.
Rows 3 and 4 Rep rows 1 and 2.
Row 5 Rep row 1.
Row 6 K10,*P5, K5, rep from * to end.
Row 7 *P5, K5, rep from * to end.
Rows 8 and 9 Rep rows 6 and 7.
Row 10 Rep row 6.
Rows 1 to 10 form block patt. Cont in patt until work meas approx 58in (147cm), ending with WS facing for next row. Break yarn A.
Join in yarn E and purl 1 row.
Bind off.

STRIP 2

Using size 5 (3.75mm) needle and yarn D, cast on 140 sts using long-tail method. Break yarn D. Join in yarn B and work in patt as folls:
Row 1 K to end.
Row 2 K5, P to end.
Rows 3 to 6 Rep rows 1 and 2 twice.
Row 7 *K3, P3, rep from * to last 8 sts, K8.
Row 8 K5, P to end.
Rows 9 to 12 Rep rows 7 and 8 twice.
Rows 13 to 18 Rep rows 1 to 6.

Row 19 *P3, K3, rep from * to last 8 sts, P3, K5.
Row 20 K5, P to end.
Rows 21 to 24 Rep rows 19 and 20 twice.
Rows 1 to 24 form patt rep. Cont in patt until work meas approx 40in (101cm), ending with row 4 or 16. Break yarn B.
Join in yarn E and knit 2 rows. Break yarn E.
Join in yarn C and work as folls:
Row 1 and alt rows K to end.
Row 2 K5, *K2, P4, rep from * to last 3 sts, K2, P1.
Row 4 Rep row 2.
Row 6 K5, P3,* K2, P4, rep from * to end.
Row 8 Rep row 6.
Rows 1 to 8 form patt rep. Cont in patt until work meas approx 58in (147cm), ending with row 1 or 5. Break yarn C.
Join in yarn E and purl 1 row.
Bind off.

FINISHING

Block pieces to measurements. With WS together (crochet is on RS as a contrast detail) and using size F/5 (3.75mm) crochet hook and yarn D, join strips with a row of single crochet to make a decorative seam. Weave in ends.

WINE/CRIMSON

Rich colors and soft yarns add warmth to the cold, dark months of the year, as log fires burn and as the autumn fruits gather on the trees. Deep reds and rich pinks blend together to create a comforting feel.

Wrapover Cardigan
Wrap up for winter in
this soft wool/cotton
yarn cardigan.
Contrasting fine stripes
of different greens
create a flash of color.
Page 48.

Following pages:
Block-striped Afghan
This afghan has an
Amish patchwork feel
to it, with its simple
blocks of colors and
stripes in wool tweed
yarn. Page 52.

Tweed Slippers
Just right for toasting
your feet by the fire,
these wool tweed
slippers are knitted on
two needles, and
embellished with cross-
stitch. Page 50.

Silk Rag Rug
This very simple piece is knitted in a tweedy silk/cotton yarn in garter-stitch stripes. The soft colors give it the feeling of a treasured rag rug. Page 53.

Garter-stitch Pillow

Nothing could be simpler than this vibrant two-tone pillow, easy to knit on big needles in chunky yarn. Page 54.

Block-striped Afghan
Team the pillow
opposite with this
Block-striped Afghan
(see page 36 for full
picture and page 52
for the pattern).

Child's Jacket
This soft cotton jacket is knitted with contrasting-colored garter-stitch borders at the hem and cuffs. It can be knitted for a boy or girl, simply by varying the color choice. This version is in cobalt blue with a soft green trim. Page 58.

Mittens
In a raspberry-colored wool/cotton yarn, with a citrus tip on the ribbing, these mittens are just right for a crisp winter's morning. Page 56.

Block-striped Scarf
Knitted in blocks of fuchsia pink and rich red, with a contrasting color at each end, this stockinette-stitch scarf is a fashionable asset to anyone's winter wardrobe. Page 55.

Cable Socks
Cable-knit patterns are great for socks as they have extra elasticity. Knitted in a wool/cotton yarn, the toes and heels are a rich burgundy, while the ribbing has pale lime-green tips.
Page 60.

Cable Hot-water Bottle Cover
This cable pattern ensures extra insulation and a snug fit to the cover. A pretty crochet picot trim makes a nice decorative finish, along with the drawstring cord in a soft, bright green. Worked in cotton yarn, it is delightfully soft and comforting.
Page 62.

Wrapover Cardigan

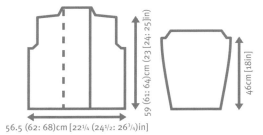

56.5 (62: 68)cm [22¼ (24½: 26¾)in]

59 (61: 64)cm (23 [24: 25]in)

46cm [18in]

SIZES & YARNS

Size	S	M	L	
To fit bust	34-38	38-42	42-46	in
	86-96	96-107	107-117	cm
Actual size	44½	49	53½	in
	113	124	136	cm
Length to shoulder	23	24	25	in
	59	61	64	cm
Sleeve length	18	18	18	in
	46	46	46	cm

Rowan Wool Cotton, 50g balls

A Burgundy (910)	17	18	19
B Olive (946)	1	1	1
C Pale lime (901)	1	1	1

NEEDLES

1 pair of size 10½ (7.5mm) needles.

2 stitch holders.

GAUGE

14 sts and 16 rows to 4in (10cm) measured over St st using size 10½ (7.5mm) needles and double (2 strands) yarn.

Note: Use 2 strands of yarn throughout.

BACK

Using size 10½ (7.5mm) needles and yarn B, cast on 79 (87: 95) sts. Break yarn B. Join in yarn A and work 7in (18cm) in St st.

Break yarn A. Join in yarn C and work 1 row.

Break yarn C. Join in yarn A and cont in St st until work meas 15 (15½: 16)in [38 (39: 40)cm], ending with RS facing for next row.

Shape armholes

Bind off 2 (3: 4) sts at beg of next 2 rows.

Row 3 K2,ssk, K to last 4 sts, K2tog, K2.

Row 4 P to end.

Rep rows 3 and 4 until 67 (71: 75) sts rem.

Cont without shaping until work meas 23 (24: 25)in [58 (61: 63)cm], ending with RS facing for next row.

Shape shoulders

Bind off 9 (10: 11) sts at beg of next 4 rows.

Leave 31 sts on holder.

LEFT FRONT

Using size 10½ (7.5mm) needles and yarn B, cast on 49 (53: 57) sts. Break yarn B.

Join in yarn A and work as folls:

Row 1 K45 (49: 53), (P1, K1) twice.

Row 2 K1, P1, K1, P to end.

Rep rows 1 and 2 until work measures 7in (18cm). Break yarn A. Join in yarn C and work 1 row. Break yarn C. Join in yarn A and cont until work meas 15 (15½: 16)in [38 (39: 40)cm], ending with RS facing for next row.

Shape armhole

Row 1 Bind off 2 (3: 4) sts, patt to end.

Row 2 Patt.

Row 3 K2, ssk, patt to end.

Rep rows 2 and 3 until 43 (45: 47) sts rem.

Cont without shaping until work meas 23 (24: 25)in [58 (61: 63)cm], ending with RS facing for next row.

Shape shoulder

Row 1 Bind off 9 (10: 11) sts, patt to end.

Row 2 Work even.

Rows 3 and 4 Rep rows 1 and 2.

Leave 25 sts on holder.

RIGHT FRONT

Work as for left front, reversing all shaping and noting **Row 1** (K1, P1) twice, K45 (49: 53).

Do NOT break yarn at end.

SLEEVES (make 2)

Using size 10½ (7.5mm) needles and yarn B, cast on 39 (41: 43) sts. Break yarn B. Join in yarn A and work in St st, inc 1 st at each end of row 11 and every foll 6th row to 59 (61: 63) sts. Cont without shaping until work meas 18in (46cm), ending with RS facing for next row.

Shape sleeve cap

Rows 1 and 2 Bind off 2 (3: 4) sts, work to end.

Row 3 K2, ssk, K to last 4 sts, K2tog, K2.

Row 4 P to end.

Rep rows 3 and 4 until 47 sts rem.

Bind off.

COLLAR

Join shoulder seams. With RS facing and using size 10½ (7.5mm) needles and yarn A, seed st 4, K21 from right front, K31 across back, K21, then seed st 4 from left front.

Work as folls:

Row 1 Seed st 4, P to last 4 sts, seed st 4.

Row 2 Seed st 4, K17, *ssk, K4, K2tog,* K23, rep from * to * again, K17, seed st 4.

Row 3 Rep row 1.

Row 4 Seed st 4, K16, *ssk, K4, K2tog,* K21, rep from * to * again, K16, seed st 4.

Work decs as set on alt rows until 69 sts rem. Cont without shaping until collar measures 8in (20cm). Bind off.

FINISHING

Block pieces to measurements. Ease sleeves into armhole and sew in place. Sew side and sleeve seams. Weave in any loose ends.

Tweed Slippers

SIZES & YARNS

Size To fit shoe size 5½-6½ (6½-7½)

Rowan Yorkshire Tweed DK, 50g balls

A Burgundy (342)	1	
B Rose pink (350)	2	

NEEDLES

1 pair of size 3 (3mm) needles.

GAUGE

27 sts and 38 rows to 4in (10cm) measured over St st using size 3 (3mm) needles.

UPPER SIDE 1

Using size 3 (3mm) needles and yarn B, cast on 3 sts (toe).

Work in St st throughout.

Row 1 K to end.

Row 2 Inc 1 st at beg of row.

Row 3 Inc 1 st at each end of row.

Row 4 Rep row 2.

Rows 5 and 6 Rep rows 3 and 4.

Row 7 Inc 1 st at end of row.

Row 8 P to end.

Row 9 Rep row 3. 13 sts.

Shaping rows **ONLY** given from this point.

Row 13 Inc 1 st at end of row.

Row 15 Inc 1 st at beg of row.

Row 17 Rep row 13.

Row 21 Inc 1 st at each end of row.

Row 27 Rep row 15. 19 sts.

Row 31 Inc 1 st at end of row.

Row 36 Inc 1 st at beg of row.

Row 41 Inc 1 st at end of row.

Row 46 Inc 1 st at beg of row.

Row 49 Inc 1 st at end of row. 24 sts.

Cont without shaping until work meas 5½ (6)in [14.5 (15.5)cm], ending with WS facing for next row.

Place marker at end of last row.**

Shape opening

Row 1 P2, P2tog, P to end.

Row 2 K to last 4 sts, K2tog, K2.

Row 3 Rep row 1.

Row 6 Rep row 2.

Row 9 Rep row 1. 19 sts.

Cont without shaping until work meas 8 (8½)in [20 (21)cm], ending with RS facing for next row.

Next row K to last 3 sts, inc, K2.

Work 3 rows more, then rep the inc row.

Cont without shaping until work meas 9½ (10)in [24 (25)cm], ending with RS facing for next row.

Shape heel

Row 1 K to last 2 sts, yf, sl1, yb, turn.

Row 2 Sl1, P to last 2 sts, P2tog.

Row 3 K to last 4 sts, yf, sl1, yb, turn.

Row 4 Sl1, P to last 2 sts, P2tog.

Bind off.

UPPER SIDE 2

Work as for side 1 to **, but reversing shaping. For example, on row 2, inc 1 st at END of row and, on row 7, inc 1 st at BEG of row.

Shape opening

Row 1 P to last 4 sts, P2tog tbl, P2.

Row 2 K2, sl1, K1, psso, K to end.

Row 3 Rep row 1.

Row 6 Rep row 2.

Row 9 Rep row 1. 19 sts.

Cont without shaping until work meas 8 (8½)in [20 (21)cm], ending with RS facing for next row.

Next row K1, inc, K to end.

Work 3 rows more, then rep the inc row.

Cont without shaping until work meas

9½ (10)in [24 (25)cm], ending with RS facing for next row.

Shape heel

Row 1 K to end.

Row 2 P2tog, P to last 2 sts, yb, sl1, yf, turn.

Row 3 Sl1, K to end.

Row 4 P2tog, P to last 4 sts, yb, sl1, yf, turn.

Row 5 Sl1, K to end.

Bind off purlwise.

SOLE

Using size 3 (3mm) needles and yarn A, cast on 7 sts (heel).

Work in St st throughout.

Row 1 K to end.

Rows 2 and 3 Cast on 2 sts at beg of row.

Row 4 Inc 1 st at each end of row.

Shaping rows **ONLY** given from this point.

Rows 7, 10, and 13 Inc 1 st at each end of row. 19 sts.

Cont without shaping until work meas 3in (7cm).

Dec 1 st at each end of next and foll 4th row.

Cont without shaping until work meas 5in (13cm), ending with RS facing for next row.

Rows 1, 7, 13, 17, and 21 Inc 1 st at each end of row. 25 sts.

Cont without shaping until work meas 8 (8½)in [20 (21)cm].

Shape toe

Rows 1, 4, 7, 10, 13, 15, and 16 Dec 1 st at each end of row. 11 sts.

Rows 17 and 18 Bind off 2 sts at beg of row, work to end.

Bind off rem 7 sts.

FINISHING

Weave in loose ends. To block, hand wash, roll in a towel to squeeze out excess water, then reshape to dry. Place WS of uppers together and, using yarn B and starting at marker, join seam with a running stitch ¼in (6mm) from edge, then work back up to marker using the same holes and forming a decorative seam. Using yarn A, work cross-stitch over the seam (see photograph). Join heel seam ¼in (6mm) from edge, in the same manner, omitting cross-stitch. Carefully pin upper to sole, WS facing, easing around heel and toe. Sew as before.

Make second slipper to match.

Block-striped Afghan

SIZE & YARNS

| Size | 52 x 65in |
| | 132 x 165cm |

Rowan Yorkshire Tweed DK, 50g balls

A Rose pink (350)	6
B Pale lime (348)	3
C Burgundy (342)	3
D Olive green (349)	3
E Red (344)	10

NEEDLES

Size 6 (4mm) circular needle at least 24in (61cm) long.
Size G/6 (4mm) crochet hook.

GAUGE

20 sts and 28 rows to 4in (10cm) measured over St st using size 6 (4mm) needles.

STRIP 1

Using size 6 (4mm) needle and yarn D, cast on 132 sts using long-tail method. Break yarn D. Join in yarn E and work as folls:
Row 1 K to end.
Row 2 K5, P to end.
These 2 rows form St st with garter-st edge.
Rep rows 1 and 2 until work meas 46in (117cm).
Break yarn E. Join in yarn D and work 1 row.
Break yarn D. Join in yarn A and cont in patt until work meas 65in (165cm), ending with WS facing for next row.
Break yarn A. Join in yarn B and work 1 row.
Bind off.

STRIP 2

Using size 6 (4mm) needle and yarn D, cast on 132 sts using long-tail method. Break yarn D. Join in yarn A and work as folls:
Row 1 K to end.
Row 2 P to last 5 sts, K5.
These 2 rows form St st with garter-st edge.
Rep rows 1 and 2, working in 5in (13cm) stripes of yarns A, B, C, D, and E until work meas 65in (165cm), ending with WS facing for next row.
Break yarn. Join in yarn B and work 1 row.
Bind off.

FINISHING

Block pieces to measurements. With WS together (crochet is on RS as a contrast detail) and using size G/6 (4mm) crochet hook and yarn E, join strips with a row of single crochet to make decorative seam. Weave in ends.

Silk Rag Rug

SIZE & YARNS

| Size | 21½in wide x 38in long |
| | 55cm wide x 97cm long |

Rowan Summer Tweed, 50g balls

A Pale gray (506)	3
B Light blue (500)	3
C Lime green (527)	3
D Light purple (525)	3
E Fuchsia (528)	3

NEEDLES

1 pair of size 8 (5mm) needles.
Medium size crochet hook.

GAUGE

16 sts and 32 rows to 4in (10cm) measured
over garter st using size 8 (5mm) needles.

SPECIAL NOTES

1. Rug is worked in garter stitch throughout.
2. When changing colors, knit in the ends; vary
the number of additional stitches to avoid a
harsh line.

RUG

Using size 8 (5mm) needles and yarn A, cast
on 88 sts and work in garter st in row and
color sequence as folls:
Row rep *Work 2 rows plus a few stitches with
first color, 4 rows plus a few stitches with
second color, then 6 rows plus a few stitches
with third color. Rep from *.
Color rep *Yarn A, yarn B, yarn C, yarn D, then
yarn E. Rep from *.
Cont until work meas 38in (97cm). Bind off.

FINISHING

Press using a warm iron over a damp cloth.
Make fringe
Cut 3 lengths of yarn 10in (25cm) long, fold in
half and use a crochet hook to pull the loop
through the end of the rug. Tuck the ends of
the tassel through the loop and pull tight.
Make 6 tassels in each color and place them in
A to E sequence in every 3rd stitch. Repeat for
other end of rug.

Garter-stitch Pillow

SIZE & YARNS

| Size | 18 x 18in |
| | 46 x 46cm |

Rowan Polar, 100g balls

A Red (641)	2
B Fuchsia (651)	2

18 x 18in (46 x 46cm) pillow form.

NEEDLES

1 pair of size 11 (8mm) needles.
4 stitch markers

GAUGE

12 sts and 16 rows to 4in (10cm) measured over St st using size 11 (8mm) needles.

PILLOW COVER

Using size 11 (8mm) needles and yarn A, cast on 56 sts. Join in yarn B and work 3 rows in K1, P1 rib. Break yarn B.
Using yarn A, change to St st. Cont in St st until work meas 10in (25cm). Place markers at each end of last row. Cont in St st until work measures 19in (48cm), ending with RS facing for next row. Break yarn A. Join in yarn B and change to garter st.
Cont in garter st until work meas 28in (71cm). Place markers at each end of row. Cont in garter st until work meas 39in (99cm), ending with WS facing for next row.
Join in yarn A and purl 1 row. Change to K1, P1 rib and work 2 rows. Break yarn A.
Using yarn B, bind off in rib.

FINISHING

Block to measurements. With RS together, fold the two ends toward the center using markers as top and bottom of pillow cover and overlapping center back of pillow cover by 4in (10cm). Sew side seams. Turn RS out. Insert pillow form.

Block-striped Scarf

SIZE & YARNS

Size	Length	Width	
	54	12	in
	137	30	cm

Rowan 4ply Soft, 50g balls

A Red (374)	3
B Pink (377)	1
C Light olive (379)	Small amount for edging detail.
D Light purple (375)	Small amount for edging detail.

NEEDLES

1 pair of size 3 (3.25mm) needles.

GAUGE

28 sts and 36 rows to 4in (10cm) measured over St st using size 3 (3.25mm) needles.

SCARF

Using size 3 (3.25mm) needles and yarn C, cast on 84 st using long-tail method. Break yarn C. Join in yarn A and work as folls:
Row 1 K to end.
Row 2 K6, P to last 6 sts, K6.

Rep rows 1 and 2 until work meas 40in (101cm), ending with row 2. Break yarn A.
Next row Join in yarn C; knit to end. Break yarn C.
Next row Join in yarn B and work as for row 2. Cont with yarn B until work meas 54in (137cm), ending with row 1. Break yarn B. Join in yarn D and purl 1 row. Bind off.

FINISHING

Block to measurements. Weave in any loose ends.

Mittens

SIZES & YARNS

Size	S-M	M-L

Rowan Wool Cotton, 50g balls

A Rose pink (943)	2	2
B Pale lime (901)	Small amount for edging.	

NEEDLES

1 pair of size 3 (3.25mm) needles.
Cable needle.

GAUGE

24 sts and 32 rows to 4in (10cm) measured
over St st using size 3 (3.25mm) needles.

RIGHT MITTEN

Cuff

Using size 3 (3.25mm) needles and yarn B,
cast on 52 sts. Break yarn B. Join in yarn A and
work twisted rib as folls.

Row 1 *P1, K2tog, do NOT slip stitch off needle
but knit into first stitch again, then slip both
stitches off needle, P1, rep from * to end.

Row 2 *K1, P2, K1, rep from * to end.

Rows 3 to 14 Rep rows 1 and 2 six times.

Row 15 Rep row 1.

Row 16 (*K1, P2, K1, rep from * once, K1, P2tog
K1), 4 times, K1, P2, K1. 48 sts.
Change to St st and work 4 rows.**

Shape gusset for thumb

Row 1 K25, pick up loop of row below and knit
into the back of it (called **mk**), K2, mk, K21.
Work 2 rows.

Row 4 P21, pick up loop of row below and purl
into the back of it (called **mp**), P4, mp, P25.
Work 2 rows.

Cont inc 2 sts on every 3rd row, working 2
extra sts between inc to row 19, (K25, mk, K14,
mk, K21). 62 sts.
Work 3 rows.

Shape thumb

Row 1 K41, turn.

Row 2 Cast on 1 st , P17, turn.

Row 3 Cast on 1 st , K18, turn.

Cont on these 18 sts until thumb meas 2in
(5cm), ending with RS facing for next row.

Next row *K1, K2tog, rep from* to end.

Next row P to end.

Next row K2tog across row.

Break yarn and thread through rem sts. Pull
tightly and secure. Sew thumb seam.
With RS facing, rejoin yarn to base of thumb.

Pick up and knit 2 sts from cast-on sts at base
of thumb, knit across rem 21 sts. 48 sts.
***Cont in St st until work meas 5 (6)in [13
(15)cm] from top of cable rib, ending with RS
facing for next row.

Shape top

Row 1 *Sl1, K1, psso, K20, K2tog, rep from *.

Row 2 P to end.

Row 3 *Sl1, K1, psso, K18, K2tog, rep from *.

Row 4 P to end.

Cont dec as set on alt rows until 24 sts rem.
Work 1 row. Bind off.
Sew top and side seam.***

LEFT MITTEN

Cast on and work to ** as for right mitten.

Shape gusset for thumb

Row 1 K21, mk, K2, mk, K25.
Work 2 rows.

Row 4 P25, mp, P4, mp, P21.
Work 2 rows.

Cont inc as set to row 19 (K21, mk, K14, mk,
K25). 62 sts.
Work 3 rows.

Shape thumb

Row 1 K37, turn.

Row 2 Cast on 1 st, P17, turn.

Row 3 Cast on 1 st, K18, turn.

Complete thumb as for right mitten.

With RS facing, rejoin yarn to base of thumb.

Pick up and knit 2 sts from cast on sts at base

of thumb, knit across rem 25 sts. 48 sts.

Work from *** to *** as on right mitten.

FINISHING

Weave in loose ends. To block, hand wash, roll

in a towel to squeeze out excess water, then

reshape and spread flat on a towel to dry.

Child's Jacket

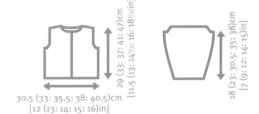

30.5 (33: 35.5: 38: 40.5)cm
[12 (13: 14: 15: 16)in]

29 (33: 37: 41: 47)cm
[11.5 (13: 14½: 16: 18½)in]

18 (23: 30.5: 35: 38)cm
[7 (9: 12: 14: 15)in]

SIZES & YARNS

	1-2	3-4	5-6	7-8	9-10	years
To fit	22	24	26	28	30	in
chest	56	61	66	71	76	cm
Actual	24	26	28	30	32	in
size	61	66	71	76	81	cm
Length to	11	12½	14	15½	18	in
shoulder	28	32	36	40	46	cm
Sleeve	7	9	12	14	15	in
length	18	23	30.5	35	38	cm

Rowan Handknit DK Cotton, 50g balls

A Blue (287)

	4	5	5	6	7

B Olive green (219)

	1	1	1	1	1
Buttons	5	5	5	7	7

NEEDLES

1 pair each of size 3 (3.25mm) and size 6 (4mm) needles.

2 safety pins.

GAUGE

20 sts and 28 rows to 4in (10cm) measured over St st using size 6 (4mm) needles.

BACK

Using size 3 (3.25mm) needles and yarn B, cast on 60 (65: 70: 75: 80) sts.

Knit 5 (5: 7: 7: 7) rows.

Break yarn B. Join in yarn A and change to size 6 (4mm) needles and St st.

Cont until work meas 6½ (7½: 8½: 9: 10)in [17 (19: 21: 23: 25)cm], ending with RS facing for next row.

Shape armholes

Bind off 2 (2: 3: 3: 4) sts at beg of next 2 rows.

Dec 1 st at each end of next and foll alt rows until 52 (55: 58: 61: 64) sts rem. Cont without shaping until work meas 11 (12½: 14: 15½: 18)in [28 (32: 36: 40: 46)cm], ending with RS facing for next row.

Shape shoulders

Sizes 1 and 2

Bind off 16 (17) sts at beg of next 2 rows.

Bind off.

Sizes 3, 4, and 5

Bind off 6 (6: 7) sts at beg of next 4 rows.

Bind off 6 (7: 6) sts at beg of next 2 rows.

Bind off.

LEFT FRONT

Using size 3 (3.25mm) needles and yarn B, cast on 34 (36: 38: 41: 43) sts.

Knit 5 (5: 7: 7: 7) rows.

Break yarn B. Join in yarn A and change to size 6 (4mm) needles and St st.

Row 1 K30 (32: 34: 37: 39), leave last 4 sts on safety pin.

Cont in St st until work measures 6½ (7½: 8½: 9: 10)in [17 (19: 21: 23: 25)cm], ending with RS facing for next row.

Shape armhole

Bind off 2 (2: 3: 3: 4) sts, K to end.

Purl 1 row.

Dec 1 st at beg of next and foll alt rows until 26 (27: 28: 30: 31) sts rem.

Cont without shaping until work is 11 (11: 7: 7: 9) rows LESS than back at shoulder, ending with WS facing for next row.

Shape neck

Sizes 1 and 2

Row 1 (WS) Bind off 5 sts, work to end.

Rows 2 to 5 Dec 1 st at neck edge.

Row 6 K to end.

Row 7 Dec 1 st at neck edge.

Rows 8 to 11 Work even.

Bind off.

Sizes 3, 4, and 5

Row 1 Bind off 5 (6: 6) sts, work to end.

Rows 2 to 5 Dec 1 st at neck edge.

Row 6 K to end.

Row 7 Dec 1 st at neck edge.

Size 5 ONLY work 2 rows in St st.

Shape shoulder

Bind off 6 (6: 7) sts at beg of next and foll alt row.

Work 1 row. Bind off rem 6 (7: 6) sts.

RIGHT FRONT

Work as for left front, reversing all shaping and starting neck 10 (10: 6: 6: 8) rows LESS than back at shoulder.

SLEEVES (make 2)

Using size 3 (3.25mm) needles and yarn B, cast on 33 (35: 37: 40: 42) sts and knit 5 (5: 7: 7: 7) rows. Break yarn B. Join in yarn A and change to size 6 (4mm) needles and St st. Inc 1 st at each end of 5th and every foll 4th (4th: 5th: 6th 6th) row to 53 (55: 59: 60: 64) sts.

Cont without shaping until work meas 7 (9: 12: 14: 15)in [18 (23: 30.5: 35: 38)cm], ending with RS facing for next row.

Shape sleeve cap

Bind off 2 (2: 3: 3: 4) sts at beg of next 2 rows. Dec 1 st at each end of next and foll alt rows until 45 (45: 47: 46: 48) sts rem. Bind off loosely.

BUTTON BAND

Using size 3 (3.25mm) needles and yarn A and with RS of left front facing, pick up loop before 4 sts on safety pin and K into back of it, K across 4 sts on safety pin. Work in K1, P1 rib until band, when slightly stretched, fits to neck of left front. Bind off. Sew band to left front. Mark positions for 5 (5, 5, 7, 7) buttons, the first ½in (1cm) from neck, the remainder at regular intervals, ending before the garter-stitch hem.

BUTTONHOLE BAND

Work as for button band, rejoining yarn with WS facing and purling across row. Make buttonholes to correspond with marked button positions as folls: Rib 1, K2tog, yo, rib2. Sew band to right front.

COLLAR

Using size 3 (3.25mm) needles and yarn A, cast on 55 (57: 61: 65: 71) sts and work in garter st for 2 (2: 2½: 2½: 2¾)in [5.5 (5.5: 6: 6.5: 7)cm]. Bind off.

FINISHING

Block pieces to measurements. Sew shoulder seams. Ease sleeves into armhole and sew in place. Sew side and sleeve seams. Starting and finishing halfway across front bands, pin bound-off edge of collar around neck, RS of collar to WS of garment. Sew in place. Weave in any loose ends. Sew on buttons.

Cable Socks

SIZES & YARNS

To fit	S - M	M - L	
Foot length	9	10	in
	24	26	cm

Rowan Wool Cotton, 50g balls

A Dusty pink (959)	4	4
B Burgundy (910)	1	1
C Pale lime (901)	Small amount for	
	edging.	

NEEDLES

4 x size 6 (4mm) double-pointed needles.
Spare needle. Cable needle.

GAUGE

22 sts and 30 rows to 4in (10cm) measured
over Cable patt using size 6 (4mm) needles.

SPECIAL ABBREVIATIONS

c4b = slip next 2 sts onto cable needle, leave
at back of work, K2, K2 from cable needle.

SOCKS

Using size 6 (4mm) needles and yarn C, cast
on 60 sts (20 sts on each of 3 needles). Break

yarn C. Join in yarn B and work 6 rounds in K1,
P1 rib. Break yarn B.

Join in yarn A and work as folls:

Rounds 1 to 4 *P2, K4, P2, K2, rep from * to end.
Round 5 *P2, c4b, P2, K2, rep from * to end.
Round 6 Rep round 1.

Rep rounds 1 to 6 until work meas approx 13in
(33cm), ending with round 6.

Next round P2, K1, K2tog, K1, P2, K2, *P2, K4,
P2, K2, rep from * twice more, *P2, K1, K2tog,
K1, P2, K2, rep from *. 57 sts.

Start heel

P2, K3, P2, K2. Break yarn A. Turn. Using
spare needle and joining in yarn B (WS facing),
P29, turn.

On these 29 sts, work 2½in (6cm) in St st,
ending with RS facing for next row.

Shape heel

Row 1 K16, K2tog tbl, K1, turn.
Row 2 Sl1, P5, P2tog, P1, turn.
Row 3 Sl1, K6, K2tog tbl, K1, turn.
Row 4 Sl1, P7, P2tog, P1, turn.

Cont as set until all sts are on 1 needle. Break
yarn B.

Next row Slip first 9 sts from heel needle to
needle 3. Needle 1: Join in yarn A and K last 8

sts from heel needle, pick up and K10 sts from
side of heel, K1 instep st; needle 2: work cable
patt as est over 26 instep sts; needle 3: K1
instep st, pick up and K10 sts from side of
heel, K first 9 heel sts. This is new beg of rnd.
(19:26:20) sts.

Shape gusset

Round 1 Needle 1: K to last 3 sts, K2tog, K1;
needle 2: Cable patt; needle 3: K1, ssk, K to
end.
Round 2 Knit around.

Rep these two rounds 5 more times. 53 sts.
(13:26:14) sts.

Cont without shaping until foot meas 7½ (8
¼) [19 (21)cm]. Break yarn A.

Shape toe

Using yarn B, work as folls:

Round 1 Needle 1: K to last 3 sts, K2tog, K1;
needle 2: K1, ssk, K to end; needle 3: K1, ssk,
K to end. 50 sts.

Round 2 Knit around.

Round 3 (dec) Needle 1: K to last 3 sts, K2tog,
K1; needle 2: K1, ssk, K to last 3 sts, K2tog, K1;
needle 3: K1, ssk, K to end. 50 sts

Rep round 3 every 3rd round 3 times, then
every other round until 26 sts rem. Turn sock

inside-out and slip sts from needle 3 to
needle 1. Close toe with 3-needle bind off.
Make second sock to match.

FINISHING

Sew bound-off edge, making a flat seam.
Weave in any loose ends. To block the socks,
hand wash, roll in a towel to squeeze out
excess water, then reshape and spread flat
to dry.

Hot-water Bottle Cover

SIZE & YARNS

Size   To fit average size
                    hot-water bottle.

Rowan Handknit DK Cotton, 50g balls

A Lilac (305)	4
B Olive green (219)	1

NEEDLES

1 pair of size 6 (4mm) needles.
1 size G/6 (4mm) crochet hook.

GAUGE

20 sts and 28 rows to 4in (10cm) measured over Cable patt using size 6 (4mm) needles.

SPECIAL ABBREVIATIONS

c6b = slip next 3 sts onto cable needle, leave at back of work, K3, K3 from cable needle.

COVER PART 1

Using size 6 (4mm) needles and yarn B, cast on 49 sts. Break yarn B. Join in yarn A and work 4 rows in K1, P1 rib.
Next row (RS) P2, *P3, inc, K1, inc, K1, rep from * to last 5 sts, P5. 61 sts.

Change to patt as folls:
Row 1 and alt rows K2, *K3, P6, rep from * to last 5 sts, K5.
Row 2 P2, *P3, K6, rep from * to last 5 sts, P5.
Row 4 P2, *P3, c6b, rep from *to last 5 sts, P5.
Row 6 Rep row 2.
Rows 1 to 6 form patt rep. Cont in patt until work meas 15½in (39cm), ending with RS facing for next row.
Shape shoulders
Row 1 K2, sl1, K1, psso, patt to last 4 sts, K2tog, K2.
Row 2 P2, P2tog, patt to last 4 sts, P2tog tbl, P2.
Row 3 K2, sl1, K1, psso, K1, K2tog, patt to last 7 sts, sl1, K1, psso, K1, K2tog, K2.
Row 4 Rep row 2.
Row 5 K2, sl1, K1, psso, K2tog, patt to last 6 sts, sl1, K1, psso, K2tog, K2.
Row 6 Rep row 2.
Row 7 K2, sl1, K1, psso, patt to last 4 sts, K2tog, K2.
Row 8 Rep row 2.
Row 9 Rep row 7.
Row 10 Rep row 2.
Row 11 K2, sl1, K1, psso, K1, K2tog, patt to last 7 sts, sl1, K1, psso, K1, K2tog, K2.
Row 12 P2, P2tog, P2tog tbl, patt to last 6 sts, P2tog, P2tog tbl, P2.
Row 13 Rep row 7.
Row 14 P2, P2tog, P3, P2tog, P1, P2tog, P4, P2tog, P1, P2tog, P2, P2tog tbl, P2. 21 sts.
Row 15 K to end.
Row 16 (make eyelet holes) P1, *P2tog, yo, P2, rep from * to end.
Work 16 rows in St st. Bind off.

COVER PART 2

Work as for cover part 1 until knitting meas 7½in (19cm), ending with same patt row as on part 1 and with RS facing for next row.
Shape shoulders as on part 1.

FINISHING

Weave in loose ends. To block, hand wash, roll in a towel to squeeze out excess water, then reshape and spread flat on a towel to dry.
Place RS together, matching shoulders and top. Fold extension of part 1 up to part 2 and overlap part 2 by 2½in (6cm). Sew side seams. Turn RS out and press using a warm iron over a damp cloth.

Make picot edging around top as folls:
Using yarn B, work a round of single crochet
around top.
Next round *1sc in each of next 3sc, then ch3
and join with a slip st to last sc to make picot,
rep from * to end.
Make drawstring by cutting 6 lengths of yarn
B, 51in (130cm) long. Tie lengths together with
a knot 3in (7cm) from one end. Make a braid,
using 2 strands for each of the 3 sections. Tie
knot at finishing end, leaving 3in (7cm) free.
Thread through eyelets of cover.

CHARCOAL/SLATE

This largely monochromatic color palette reflects the clear silhouettes of the winter landscape. The minimalist look is softened by the use of luxury yarns with interesting textures. Beat the elements with cozy sweaters and soft afghans and pillows.

Tweed sweater
(opposite)
This comfortable
turtleneck sweater with
cable ribs is great for
everyone, of any age,
male or female.
Page 76.

Left: The Blanket
Cardigan (also shown
on page 71) and the
Half-and-half and
Folding Pillows (shown
on pages 72 and 73) are
great for winter picnics
on the beach.

Half-and-half and Tweed Afghans

Two versatile afghans to knit: use them as throws, bed covers, or winter wraps. The Half-and-half Afghan (far left and opposite) is knitted in two pieces and grafted together using a simple crochet stitch. The Tweed Afghan (left) is knitted in two shades of gray wool tweed yarn, trimmed in black.

Blanket cardigan
(page 71)
This is a versatile garment; dress it up for evenings, or wrap it around you for a walk on the beach. Page 80.

Half-and-half Pillow
A simple but very graphic pillow design, knitted in two colors of a wool/cotton yarn, with a rib closure providing a feature on the reverse side. Page 84.

Folding Pillow
One of the easiest designs to knit, this soft, fluffy mohair pillow goes well with the Half-and-half Pillow. Page 83.

Tweed Pillow
A single row of contasting color sets off the monochromatic blocks of color on this warm wool pillow. Page 82.

Half-and-half and Tweed Afghans
Seeing them close up, you can appreciate the textural effect of these wonderfully graphic afghans. See also pages 68 and 69, and patterns on pages 78 and 79.

Tweed Sweater

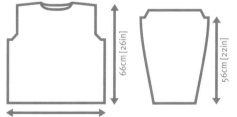

56 (61: 66)cm [22 (24: 26)in]

SIZES & YARNS

Size	S	M	L	
To fit chest	40	44	48	in
	102	112	122	cm
Actual size	44	48	52	in
	112	122	132	cm
Length to shoulder	25	25	25	in
	64	64	64	cm
Sleeve length	22	22	22	in
	56	56	56	cm

Rowan Yorkshire Tweed 4ply, 25g balls

A Mid gray (270)	26	28	30
B Charcoal gray (277)	1	1	1

NEEDLES

1 pair each of size 7 (4.5mm) and size 8 (5mm) needles.
Cable needle.
2 stitch holders.

GAUGE

19 sts and 26 rows to 4in (10cm) measured over St st using size 8 (5mm) needles and double (2 strands) yarn.

SPECIAL ABBREVIATIONS

c4b = slip next 2 sts onto cable needle, leave at back of work, K2, K2 from cable needle.

Note: Use 2 strands of yarn throughout.

BACK

Using size 7 (4.5mm) needles and yarn B, cast on 106 (116: 126) sts. Break yarn B and join in yarn A.
Work in cable rib as folls:
Row 1 P1 (0: K2),*P2, K4, rep from * to last 3 (2: 4) sts, P2, P1 (0: K2).
Row 2 K1 (0: P2), *K2, P4, rep from * to last 3 (2: 4) sts, K2, K1 (0: P2).
Rows 3 and 4 Rep rows 1 and 2.
Row 5 P1 (0: K2), *P2, c4b, rep from * to last 3 (2: 4) sts, P2, P1 (0: K2).
Row 6 Rep row 2.
Rows 1 to 6 form cable rib patt.
Rows 7 to 18 Rep rows 1 to 6 twice.
Change to size 8 (5mm) needles and St st.
Cont until work measures 16in (41cm).
Shape armholes
Rows 1 and 2 Bind off 3 (3: 4) sts, work to end.
Row 3 K2, ssk, K to last 4 sts, K2tog, K2.

Row 4 P to end.
Rep rows 3 and 4 until 94 (102: 108) sts rem.
Cont without shaping until work meas 25in (64cm).
Shape shoulders and neck
Rows 1 and 2 Bind off 8 (8: 9) sts, K to end.
Row 3 Bind off 8 (8: 9) sts, K19 (23: 24), turn.
Row 4 Bind off 4 sts, P to end.
Row 5 Bind off 8 (9: 9) sts, K to end.
Row 6 Bind off 0 (1: 2) sts, P to end.
Bind off.
Place center 24 sts on stitch holder. RS facing, rejoin yarn to rem sts at neck edge and work to match, reversing shaping.

FRONT

Work as for back until front meas 24in (61.5cm).
Shape neck and shoulders
Row 1 K38 (41: 43), turn. Put rem sts on holder.
Rows 2 to 5 Dec 1 st at neck edge.
Row 6 P to end.
Row 7 Bind off 8 (8: 9) sts, K to last 2 sts, K2tog.
Row 8 P to end.
Rows 9 and 10 As rows 7 and 8.
Row 11 Bind off 8 (9: 9) sts, work to last 2 sts, K2tog.

Row 12 P to end.
Bind off.
Place center 18 (20: 22) sts on stitch holder. RS facing, rejoin yarn to rem sts and work to match first side of neck, reversing shaping.

SLEEVES (make 2)

Using yarn B and size 7 (4.5mm) needles, cast on 50 (50: 56) sts. Break yarn B and join in yarn A. Work 18 rows in cable rib as for 2nd (medium) size back.
Change to size 8 (5mm) needles and St st. Inc 1 st at each end of every foll 6th row to 86 (86: 88) sts. Cont without shaping until work meas 22in (56cm).
Shape sleevecap
Bind off 3 (3: 4) sts at beg of next 2 rows.
Row 3 K2, ssk, K to last 4 sts, K2tog, K2.
Row 4 P to end.
Rep rows 3 and 4 until 64 sts rem. Bind off.

TURTLENECK COLLAR

Sew right shoulder seam. With RS facing and using size 7 (4.5mm) needles and yarn A, pick up and K15 sts down left front neck, knit across 18 (20: 22) sts on holder, pick up and K15 sts up right front neck, K6 (7: 8) sts from right back neck, knit across 24 sts on holder, pick up and K6 (7: 8) sts from left back neck. 84 (88: 92) sts.
Work 7in (18cm) in K2, P2 rib. Bind off loosely in rib.

FINISHING

Block pieces to measurements. Sew right shoulder seam. Sew collar seam with RS facing at base half and with WS facing at top half so that seam is not visible when folded over. Ease sleeves into armholes and sew in place. Sew side and sleeve seams. Weave in loose ends.

Half-and-half Afghan

SIZE & YARNS

| Size | 47 x 64in |
| | 120 x 162cm |

Rowan Wool Cotton, 50g balls

| A Gray (903) | 10 |
| B Black (908) | 10 |

NEEDLES

Size 6 (4mm) circular needle at least 24in (61cm) long.
Size G/6 (4mm) crochet hook.

GAUGE

22 sts and 30 rows to 4in (10cm) measured over St st using size 6 (4mm) needle.

STRIP 1

Using size 6 (4mm) needle and yarn A, cast on 132 sts using long-tail method. Break yarn A. Join in yarn B and work as folls:
Row 1 (K1, P1) twice, K to end.
Row 2 P to last 5 sts, (K1, P1) twice, K1.
These 2 rows form St st with seed st edge.
Rep rows 1 and 2 until work meas 64in (162cm), ending with row 2 and RS facing for next row. Bind off.

STRIP 2

Using size 6 (4mm) needle and yarn A, cast on 132 sts using long-tail method.
Row 1 K to last 5 sts, (P1, K1) twice, P1.
Row 2 (P1, K1) twice, P to end.
These 2 rows form St st with seed st edge.
Rep rows 1 and 2 until work is 1 row less than strip 1 at bound-off edge, ending with WS facing for next row. Break yarn A.
Join in yarn B and work row 2. Bind off.

FINISHING

Block pieces to measurements. With WS together (crochet is on RS as a contrast detail) and using size G/6 (4mm) crochet hook and yarn A, join strips with a row of single crochet to make decorative seam. Weave in ends.

Tweed Blanket

SIZE & YARNS

| Size | 51 x 68in |
| | 131 x 172cm |

Rowan Yorkshire Tweed 4ply, 25g balls

A Charcoal gray (277)	34
B Mid gray (270)	16
C Black (283)	1

NEEDLES

Size 8 (5mm) circular needle at least 24in (61cm) long.
Size G/6 (4mm) crochet hook.

GAUGE

19 sts and 26 rows to 4in (10cm) measured over St st using size 8 (5mm) needle and double (2 strands) yarn.
Note: Use 2 strands of yarn throughout.

STRIP 1

Using size 8 (5mm) needle and yarn B, cast on 124 sts using long-tail method. Break yarn B. Join in yarn A and work as folls:
Row 1 K to end.
Row 2 P to last 5 sts, K5.

These 2 rows form St st with garter-st edge.
Cont as set until work meas 48in (122cm), ending with row 1. Break yarn A.
Join in yarn C and work row 2. Break yarn C.
Join in yarn B and rep rows 1 and 2 until work meas 68in (172cm), ending with row 1. Break yarn B.
Join in yarn C and purl 1 row.
Bind off.

STRIP 2

Using size 8 (5mm) needle and yarn B, cast on 124 sts using long-tail method. Break yarn B, join in yarn A and work colors as for strip 1 but note:
Row 1 K to end.
Row 2 K5, P to end.
Work as strip 1.

FINISHING

Block pieces to measurements. With WS together (crochet is on RS as a contrast detail) and using 2 strands of yarn A and size G/6 (4mm) crochet hook, join strips with a row of single crochet to make decorative seam.
Weave in ends.

Blanket Cardigan

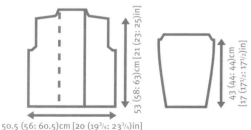

50.5 (56: 60.5)cm [20 (19³/₄: 23³/₄)in]

53 (58: 63)cm [21 (23: 25)]in

43 (44: 44)cm [17 (17¹/₂: 17¹/₂)]in

SIZES & YARNS

Size	S	M	L	
To fit bust	34-36	36-38	40-44	in
	86-91	91-96	102-112	cm
Actual size	39½	44	47½	in
	101	112	121	cm
Length to shoulder	20½	22½	24½	in
	52	57	62	cm
Sleeve length	17	17½	17½	in
	43	44	44	cm

Rowan Wool Cotton, 50g balls

A Black (908)	10	11	12
B Gray (903)	1	1	1

NEEDLES

1 pair of size 6 (4mm) needles.
3 stitch holders.

GAUGE

22 sts and 30 rows to 4in (10cm) measured over St st using size 6 (4mm) needles.

BACK

Using size 6 (4mm) needles and yarn B, cast on 111 (123: 133) sts.

Break yarn B and join in yarn A.
Work 45 rows in St st.
Break yarn A. Join in yarn B and purl 1 row.
Break yarn B. Join in yarn A and cont in St st until work meas 12½ (14: 15½)in [32 (36: 40)cm].

Shape armholes

Bind off 3 (4: 5) sts at beg of next 2 rows.
Row 3 K2, ssk, K to last 4 sts, K2tog, K2.
Row 4 P to end.
Rep rows 3 and 4 until 95 (103: 109) sts rem.
Cont without shaping until work meas 20½ (22½: 24½)in [52 (57: 62)cm], ending with RS facing for next row.

Shape shoulders

Rows 1 to 4 Bind off 8 (9: 10) sts, work to end.
Rows 5 and 6 Bind off 7 (8: 9) sts, work to end.
Leave rem 49 (51: 51) sts on holder.

LEFT FRONT

Using size 6 (4mm) needles and yarn B, cast on 73 (78: 83) sts.
Break yarn B.
Join in yarn A and work as folls:
Row 1 K68 (73: 78), (P1, K1) twice, P1.

Row 2 (P1, K1) twice, P to end.
Rows 1 and 2 form St st with seed st border.
Rows 3 to 44 Rep rows 1 and 2.
Row 45 Rep row 1.
Break yarn A.
Row 46 Join in yarn B, work as row 2.
Break yarn B.
Join in yarn A and cont in St st with seed st edging until work measures 12½ (14: 15½)in [32 (36: 40)cm], ending with RS facing for next row.

Shape armhole

Row 1 Bind off 3 (4: 5) sts, patt to end.
Row 2 Patt to end.
Row 3 K2, ssk, patt to end.
Rep rows 2 and 3 until 65 (68: 71) sts rem.
Cont without shaping until work meas 20½ (22½: 24½)in [52 (57: 62)cm], ending with RS facing for next row.

Shape shoulder

Row 1 Bind off 8 (9: 10) sts, patt to end.
Rows 2 Patt to end.
Rows 3 and 4 Rep rows 1 and 2.
Row 5 Bind off 7 (8: 9) sts, patt to end.
Row 6 Patt to end.
Leave rem 42 sts on holder.

RIGHT FRONT

Work as for left front, reversing all shaping and OMITTING the row in yarn B. Do NOT break yarn at end.

SLEEVES (make 2)

Using size 6 (4mm) needles and yarn B, cast on 51 (55: 61) sts. Break yarn B. Join in yarn A. Change to St st and inc 1 st at each end of row 7 and every foll 8th row to 79 (83: 87) sts. Cont until work measures 17 (17½: 17½)in [43 (44: 44)cm], ending with RS facing for next row.

Shape sleeve cap

Rows 1 and 2 Bind off 3 (4: 5) sts, work to end. Work decs as on back until 63 (69: 71) sts rem. Work 1 row.
Bind off.

COLLAR

Sew shoulder seams. With RS facing and using size 6 (4mm) needles and yarn A, seed st across right front edging, K37, K49 (51: 51) across back, K37, seed st 5 from left front. 133 (135: 135) sts.
Work as folls:

Row 1 Seed st 5, P to last 5 sts, seed st to end.
Row 2 Seed st 5, K33, *ssk, K4, K2tog,* K41 (43: 43), rep from * to * again, K33, seed st 5.
Row 3 Rep row 1
Row 4 Seed st 5, K32, *ssk, K4, K2tog,* K39 (41: 41), rep from * to * again, K32, seed st 5.
Work dec as set on alt rows until 113 (115: 115) sts rem. Cont without shaping until collar measures 8in (20cm).
Bind off.

FINISHING

Block pieces to measurements. Ease sleeves into armhole and sew in place. Sew side and sleeve seams. Weave in any loose ends.

Tweed Pillow

SIZE & YARNS

Size   18 x 18in
                        46 x 46cm

Rowan Yorkshire Tweed 4ply, 25g balls

A Charcoal gray (277)	6
B Mid gray (270)	5
C Black (283)	1

18 x 18in (46 x 46cm) pillow form.

NEEDLES

1 pair of size 8 (5mm) needles.
4 stitch markers.

GAUGE

19 sts and 26 rows to 4in (10cm) measured
over St st using size 8 (5mm) needles and
double (2 strands) yarn.
Note: Use 2 strands of yarn throughout.

PILLOW COVER

Using size 8 (5mm) needles and yarn C, cast
on 91 sts. Break yarn C. Join in yarn B and knit
1 row. Change to K1, P1 rib and work 3 rows.
Change to St st and cont until work meas 12in
(30cm). Place markers at each end of last row.

Cont in St st until work meas 18in (46cm).
Break yarn B.
Join in yarn C and work 1 row. Break yarn C.
Join in yarn A and cont in St st until work meas
30in (76cm). Place markers at each end of
last row.
Cont in St st until work meas 39in (99cm),
ending with WS facing for next row.
Change to K1, P1 rib and work 4 rows. Break
yarn A.
Join in yarn B and purl 1 row.
Bind off.

FINISHING

Block to measurements. With RS together, fold
the two ends toward the center, using markers
as top and bottom of pillow cover, and
overlapping center back of pillow cover by 4in
(10cm). Sew side seams. Turn RS out. Insert
pillow form.

Folding Pillow

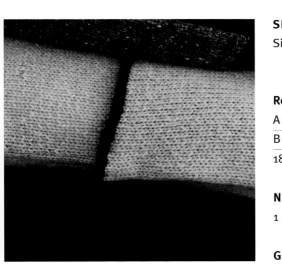

SIZE & YARNS

| Size | 18 x 18in |
| | 46 x 46cm |

Rowan Kid Classic, 50g balls

A Pale gray (840)	4
B Charcoal gray (831)	1

18 x 18in (46 x 46cm) pillow form.

NEEDLES

1 pair of size 8 (5mm) needles.

GAUGE

19 sts and 25 rows to 4in (10cm) measured over St st using size 8 (5mm) needles.

PILLOW COVER

Front and back (both alike)
Using size 8 (5mm) needles and yarn B, cast on 86 sts and knit 1 row. Break yarn B. Join in yarn A and, starting with a **K** row, work 28in (71cm) in St st, ending with a WS row.
Bind off.

FINISHING

Block to measurements. Place bound-off edges together, RS facing. Sew side seams and bound-off edges. Turn RS out. Insert pillow form. Fold over excess knitting as decorative detail.

Half-and-half Pillow

SIZE & YARNS

| Size | 18 x 18in |
| | 46 x 46cm |

Rowan Wool Cotton, 50g balls

A Black (908)	3
B Gray (903)	2

18 x 18in (46 x 46cm) pillow form.

NEEDLES

1 pair of size 5 (3.75mm) needles.
4 stitch markers.

GAUGE

24 sts and 32 rows to 4in (10cm) measured
over St st using size 5 (3.75mm) needles.

PILLOW COVER

Using size 5 (3.75mm) needles and yarn A,
cast on 111 sts. Join in yarn B and knit 1 row.
Change to K1, P1 rib and work 5 rows. Break
yarn B.
Using yarn A, change to St st and cont until
work meas 12in (30cm). Place markers at each
end of last row.
Cont in St st until work meas 21in (53cm).

Break yarn A.
Join in yarn B and cont in St st until work meas
30in (76cm). Place markers at each end of
last row.
Cont in St st until work meas 39in (99cm),
ending with WS facing for next row.
Join in yarn A and purl 1 row. Change to K1, P1
rib and work 5 rows. Break yarn A.
Using yarn B, purl 1 row.
Bind off.

FINISHING

Block to measurements. With RS together, fold
the two ends toward the center, using markers
as top and bottom of pillow cover, and
overlapping center back of pillow cover by 4in
(10cm). Sew side seams. Turn RS out.
Insert pillow form.

LIME/LILAC

Child's Jacket

Cotton is just right for breezy summer days. This comfortable classic pattern has garter-stitch hems and borders, knitted in a softly contrasting color, and is ideal for young children. Page 100.

Fresh, clear colors, in which the softness of lilac and lavender is offset by the sharp acidity of lime and lemon, are ideal for the summer months. White adds purity and calmness to the palette, and the different qualities of cotton yarns emphasize the texture perfectly.

Lace Shawl
Gossamer light in a faded, soft, fluffy yarn, this delicate shawl makes the perfect evening cover-up for a summer's night. Page 102.

Cable Afghan

Richly textured, this white cable-stitch cotton afghan has garter-stitch borders edged in soft lilac. Page 103.

Three-textured Pillow

Alternating colors and textures create a quirky visual impact in this, the third pillow in the group. Put all three together, as here, to mix and match.
Page 106.

Garter-check Pillow

A soft medium-weight cotton yarn, knit in two different garter-stitch textures, creates a great summer pillow.
Page 104.

Garter-stripe Pillow

The fine quality of this garter-stitch pattern pillow in pure white with lavender details makes it perfect for the bedroom, too.
Page 105.

Seed-stitch Camisole
This little seed-stitch camisole is trimmed with a crochet picot edge in deep lavender. The ribbon detail makes it just right for a warm summer day. Page 107.

Laundry Bag

Practical but beautiful, this laundry bag has a Victorian feel; it is knitted in lightweight cotton yarn in a delicate seed-stitch diamond pattern, and trimmed with a crochet picot edge and drawstring cord in deep lavender. Page 108.

Wash Bag

Make a matching wash bag in the same yarn and stitch pattern, but in deep lavender with pale lime trim and drawstring. Page 109.

Child's Jacket

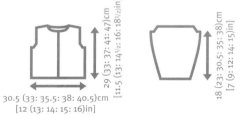

30.5 (33: 35.5: 38: 40.5)cm
[12 (13: 14: 15: 16)in]

29 (33: 37: 41: 47)cm
[11.5 (13: 14½: 16: 18½)in]

18 (23: 30.5: 35: 38)cm
[7 (9: 12: 14: 15)in]

SIZES & YARNS

	1-2	3-4	5-6	7-8	9-10	years
To fit	22	24	26	28	30	in
chest	56	61	66	71	76	cm
Actual	24	26	28	30	32	in
size	61	66	71	76	81	cm
Length to	11	12½	14	15½	18	in
shoulder	28	32	36	40	46	cm
Sleeve	7	9	12	14	15	in
length	18	23	30.5	35	38	cm

Rowan Handknit DK Cotton, 50g balls

A Lilac (305)

4	5	5	6	7

B Blue (287)

1	1	1	1	1

Buttons 5 | 5 | 5 | 7 | 7 |

NEEDLES

1 pair each of size 3 (3.25mm) and size 6 (4mm) needles.
2 safety pins.

GAUGE

20 sts and 28 rows to 4in (10cm) measured over St st using size 6 (4mm) needles.

BACK

Using size 3 (3.25mm) needles and yarn B, cast on 60 (65: 70: 75: 80) sts.

Knit 5 (5: 7: 7: 7) rows.

Break yarn B. Join in yarn A and change to size 6 (4mm) needles and St st.

Cont until work meas 6½ (7½: 8½: 9: 10)in [17 (19: 21: 23: 25)cm], ending with RS facing for next row.

Shape armholes

Bind off 2 (2: 3: 3: 4) sts at beg of next 2 rows.

Dec 1 st at each end of next and foll alt rows until 52 (55: 58: 61: 64) sts rem. Cont without shaping until work meas 11 (12½: 14: 15½: 18)in [28 (32: 36: 40: 46)cm], ending with RS facing for next row.

Shape shoulders

Sizes 1 and 2

Bind off 16 (17) sts at beg of next 2 rows.

Bind off.

Sizes 3, 4, and 5

Bind off 6 (6: 7) sts at beg of next 4 rows.

Bind off 6 (7: 6) sts at beg of next 2 rows.

Bind off.

LEFT FRONT

Using size 3 (3.25mm) needles and yarn B, cast on 34 (36: 38: 41: 43) sts.

Knit 5 (5: 7: 7: 7) rows.

Break yarn B. Join in yarn A and change to size 6 (4mm) needles and St st.

Row 1 K30 (32: 34: 37: 39), leave last 4 sts on safety pin.

Cont in St st until work measures 6½ (7½: 8½: 9: 10)in [17 (19: 21: 23: 25)cm], ending with RS facing for next row.

Shape armhole

Bind off 2 (2: 3: 3: 4) sts, K to end.

Purl 1 row.

Dec 1 st at beg of next and foll alt rows until 26 (27: 28: 30: 31) sts rem.

Cont without shaping until work is 11 (11: 7: 7: 9) rows LESS than back at shoulder, ending with WS facing for next row.

Shape neck

Sizes 1 and 2

Row 1 WS facing, bind off 5 sts, work to end.

Rows 2 to 5 Dec 1 st at neck edge.

Row 6 K to end.

Row 7 Dec 1 st at neck edge.

Rows 8 to 11 St st.

Bind off.

Sizes 3, 4, and 5

Row 1 Bind off 5 (6: 6) sts, work to end.

Rows 2 to 5 Dec 1 st at neck edge.

Row 6 K to end.

Row 7 Dec 1 st at neck edge.

Size 5 ONLY work 2 rows in St st.

Shape shoulder

Bind off 6 (6: 7) sts at beg of next and foll alt row.

Work 1 row. Bind off rem 6 (7: 6) sts.

RIGHT FRONT

Work as for left front, reversing all shaping and starting neck 10 (10: 6: 6: 8) rows LESS than back at shoulder.

SLEEVES (make 2)

Using size 3 (3.25mm) needles and yarn B, cast on 33 (35: 37: 40: 42) sts and knit 5 (5: 7: 7: 7) rows. Break yarn B. Join in yarn A and change to size 6 (4mm) needles and St st. Inc 1 st at each end of 5th and every foll 4th (4th: 5th: 6th 6th) row to 53 (55: 59: 60: 64) sts.

Cont without shaping until work meas 7 (9: 12: 14: 15)in [18 (23: 30.5: 35: 38)cm], ending with RS facing for next row.

Shape sleeve cap

Bind off 2 (2: 3: 3: 4) sts at beg of next 2 rows. Dec 1 st at each end of next and foll alt rows until 45 (45: 47: 46: 48) sts rem. Bind off loosely.

BUTTON BAND

Using size 3 (3.25mm) needles and yarn A and with RS of left front facing, pick up loop before 4 sts on safety pin and K into back of it, K across 4 sts on safety pin. Work in K1, P1 rib until band, when slightly stretched, fits to neck of left front. Bind off. Sew band to left front. Mark positions for 5 (5, 5, 7, 7) buttons, the first ½in (1cm) from neck, the remainder at regular intervals, ending before the garter-stitch hem.

BUTTONHOLE BAND

Work as for button band, rejoining yarn with WS facing and purling across row. Make buttonholes to correspond with marked button positions as folls: Rib 1, K2 tog, yo, rib 2. Sew band to right front.

COLLAR

Using size 3 (3.25mm) needles and yarn A, cast on 55 (57: 61: 65: 71) sts and work in garter st for 2 (2: 2½: 2½: 2¾)in [5.5 (5.5: 6: 6.5: 7)cm]. Bind off.

FINISHING

Block pieces to measurements. Sew shoulder seams. Ease sleeves into armholes and sew in place. Sew side and sleeve seams. Starting and finishing halfway across front bands, pin bound-off edge of collar around neck, RS of collar to WS of garment. Sew in place. Weave in any loose ends. Sew on buttons.

Lace Shawl

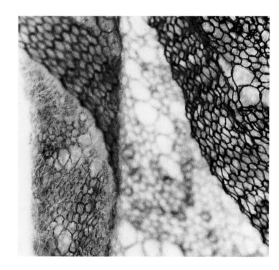

SIZE & YARNS

| Size | 49 x 49in |
| | 124 x 124cm |

Rowan Kidsilk Haze, 25g balls

| A Grape (600) | 9 |
| B Olive green (597) | Small amount for edging. |

NEEDLES

Sizes 6 (4mm) and 8 (5mm) circular needles at least 24in (61cm) long.

GAUGE

23 sts to 4in (10cm) wide measured over pattern using size 6 (4mm) needles after blocking.

SHAWL

Using size 8 (5mm) needle and yarn B, cast on 285 sts using long-tail method. Break yarn B. Join in yarn A and change to size 6 (4mm) needles and work lace patt as folls.

Row 1 (RS) K6, *K2, sl1, K1, psso, K4, K2tog, K2, yo, K1, yo, rep from * to last 6 sts, K6.

Row 2 and alt rows K6, P to last 6 sts, K6.

Row 3 K6, *yo, K2, sl1, K1, psso, K2, K2tog, K2, yo, K3, rep from * to last 6 sts, K6.

Row 5 K6, *K1, yo, K2, sl1, K1, psso, K2tog, K2, yo, K4, rep from * to last 6 sts, K6.

Row 7 K6, *yo, K1, yo, K2, sl1, K1, psso, K4, K2tog, K2, rep from * to last 6 sts, K6.

Row 9 K6, *K3, yo, K2, sl1, K1, psso, K2, K2tog, K2, yo, rep from * to last 6 sts, K6.

Row 11 K6, *K4, yo, K2, sl1, K1, psso, K2tog, K2, yo, K1, rep from * to last 6 sts, K6.

Row 12 Rep row 2.

Rows 1 to 12 form lace patt.

Rep rows 1 to 12 until work meas 49in (124cm), ending with WS row facing for next row. Break yarn A.

Join in yarn B and purl 1 row.

Change to size 8 (5mm) needles and bind off loosely.

FINISHING

Weave in any loose ends. Block to measurements.

Cable Afghan

SIZE & YARNS

| Size | 33 x 48in |
| | 84 x 122cm |

Rowan Handknit DK Cotton, 50g balls

| A White (263) | 14 |
| B Lilac (305) | 1 |

NEEDLES

Size 7 (4.5mm) circular needle at least 24in (61cm) long.
Cable needle.

GAUGE

19 sts and 26 rows to 4in (10cm) measured over cable patt using size 7 (4.5mm) needle.

SPECIAL ABBREVIATIONS

c4b = slip next 2 sts onto cable needle, leave at back of work, K2, K2 from cable needle.

AFGHAN

Using size 7 (4.5mm) needle and yarn B, cast on 159 sts. Break yarn B. Join in yarn A and knit 8 rows.
Change to cable patt as folls:

Row 1 (RS) K5, *P1, K4, P1, K5, rep from * to end.
Row 2 (and all WS rows) K6, *P4, K1, P5, K1, rep from * to last 10 sts, P4, K6.
Row 3 K5, *P1, c4b, P1, K5, rep from * to end.
Row 5 K5, *P1, K4, P6; rep from * to last 11 sts, P1, K4, P1, K5.
Rows 1 to 6 form cable patt with garter-st edge.
Rep cable patt until work meas 47in (120cm), ending with row 6. Knit 9 rows. Break yarn A.
Join in yarn B and purl 1 row.
Bind off.

FINISHING

Block to measurements. Weave in any loose ends.

Garter-check Pillow

SIZE & YARNS

| Size | 18 x 18in |
| | 46 x 46cm |

Rowan Handknit DK Cotton, 50g balls

| A Lilac (305) | 6 |
| B Olive green (219) | 1 |

18 x 18in (46 x 46cm) pillow form.

NEEDLES

1 pair each of size 5 (3.75mm) and size 6 (4mm) needles.

GAUGE

20 sts and 28 rows to 4in (10cm) measured over St st using size 6 (4mm) needles.

PILLOW COVER

Using size 5 (3.75mm) needles and yarn A, cast on 92 sts. Join in yarn B and work 6 rows in K1, P1 rib. Break yarn B.
Change to size 6 (4mm) needles, yarn A and St st. Work patt 1 as folls:
Rows 1 to 6 St st.
Row 7 K1, *K3, P3, rep from * to last st, K1.
Row 8 P to end.

Rows 9 to 12 Rep rows 7 and 8 twice.
Rows 13 to 18 St st.
Row 19 K1, *P3, K3, rep from * to last st, K1.
Row 20 P to end.
Rows 21 to 24 Rep rows 19 and 20 twice.
Rows 1 to 24 form patt rep. Work 4 more repeats, then rows 1 to 18 again. 138 rows in patt 1.
Join in yarn B and knit 2 rows. Break yarn B. Using yarn A, work patt 2 as folls.
Rows 1 and 2 St st.
Row 3 K2, *P2, K4, rep from * to end.
Row 4 P to end.
Rows 5 and 6 Rep rows 3 and 4.
Row 7 K1, *K4, P2, rep from * to last st, K1.
Row 8 P to end.
Rows 9 and 10 Rep rows 7 and 8.
Rows 3 to 10 form patt rep. Rep rows 3 to 10 until work measures approx 38½in (98cm), ending with row 6 or 10.
Next row K to end.
Join in yarn B, change to size 5 (3.75mm) needles and purl 1 row.
Work 6 rows in K1, P1 rib.
Break yarn B.
Using yarn A, bind off in rib.

FINISHING

Block to measurements. Measure 11¾in (30cm) from cast-on edge, place pins to mark first fold. Measure a further 18in (46cm) and place pins to mark 2nd fold.
Placing RS together, make first fold, then 2nd fold, overlapping at center back of cushion cover by 4in (10cm). Sew side seams. Turn RS out. Insert pillow form.

Garter-stripe Pillow

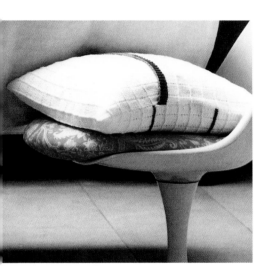

SIZE & YARNS

| Size | 18 x 18in |
| | 46 x 46cm |

Rowan Cotton Glace, 50g balls

A White (726)	6
B Lavender (787)	1
C Olive green (814)	Small amount.

18 x 18in (46 x 46cm) pillow form.

NEEDLES

1 pair each of size 3 (3.25mm) and size 5 (3.75mm) needles.
4 stitch markers.

GAUGE

23 sts and 32 rows to 4in (10cm) measured over St st using size 5 (3.75mm) needles.

PILLOW COVER

Using size 3 (3.25mm) needles and yarn C, cast on 104 sts. Break yarn C. Join in yarn B and work 6 rows in K1, P1 rib. Break yarn B. Change to size 5 (3.75mm) needles and join in yarn A. Work in patt as folls:
Row 1 K to end.
Row 2 *P6, K1, rep from * to last 6 sts, P6.
Rows 3 to 8 Rep rows 1 and 2 three times.
Rows 9 and 10 K to end.
Rows 1 to 10 form patt rep. Cont in patt until work meas 12in (30cm). Place markers at each end of last row. Cont until work meas approx 18in (46cm), ending with row 8. Join in yarn B. Knit 2 rows. Break yarn B.
Using yarn A, work rows 1 to 10 four times, then rows 1 to 8 again. Join in yarn C and knit 2 rows. Break yarn C.
Using yarn A, cont in patt until work meas 30in (76cm). Place markers at each end of last row.
Cont until work meas approx 39in (99cm), ending with row 8. Break yarn A.
Change to size 3 (3.25mm) needles and join in yarn B. Knit 1 row. Work 5 rows in K1, P1 rib. Break yarn B. Join in yarn C and bind off in rib.

FINISHING

Block to measurements. With RS together fold two ends toward center, using markers as top and bottom of cover, and overlapping center back of cover by 4in (10cm). Sew side seams. Turn RS out. Insert pillow form.

Three-textured Pillow

SIZE & YARNS

| Size | 18 x 18in |
| | 46 x 46cm |

Rowan Cotton Glace, 50g balls

A Pale lime (813)	3
B Lavender (787)	1
C Lilac (811)	1
D Olive green (814)	3

18 x 18in (46 x 46cm) pillow form.

NEEDLES

1 pair each of size 3 (3.25) and size 5 (3.75mm) needles.
4 stitch markers.

GAUGE

23 sts and 32 rows to 4in (10cm) measured over St st using size 5 (3.75mm) needles.

PILLOW COVER

Using size 3 (3.25mm) needles and yarn A, cast on 104 sts.
Join in yarn B and work 7 rows in K1, P1 rib. Break yarn B.
Change to size 5 (3.75mm) needles and yarn A.
Purl 1 row.
Work in patt as folls:
Row 1 K2, *K5, (P1, K1) twice, P1, rep from * to last 2 sts, K2.
Row 2 K2, P1, *K1, P1, K1, P7, rep from * to last st, K1.
Rows 3 to 8 Rep rows 1 and 2 three times.
Row 9 K2, *(P1, K1) twice, P1, K5, rep from * to last 2 sts, K2.
Row 10 K1, *P7, K1, P1, K1, rep from * to last 3 sts, P2, K1.
Rows 11 to 16 Rep rows 9 and 10 three times.
Rows 1 to 16 form patt rep. Cont in patt until work meas 12in (30cm). Place markers at each end of last row. Cont in patt until work meas approx 18in (46cm), ending with row 8 or 16. Break yarn A.
Join in yarn B and knit 2 rows. Break yarn B.
Join in yarn C and knit 1 row.
Change to seed stitch and cont until work meas 24in (61cm), ending with RS facing for next row. Break yarn C.
Join in yarn B and knit 2 rows. Break yarn B.
Join in yarn D and knit 1 row.
Change to patt as folls:
Row 1 K1, *P7, K1, P1, K1, rep from * to last 3 sts, P2, K1.
Row 2 K2, *(P1, K1) twice, P1, K5, rep from * to last 2 sts, K2.
Rows 1 and 2 form patt rep. Cont in patt until work measures 30in (76cm). Place markers at each end of last row. Cont until work meas approx 39in (99cm), ending with row 1. Break yarn D.
Change to size 3 (3.25mm) needles, join in yarn B and knit 1 row. Work 6 rows in K1, P1 rib. Break yarn B. Join in yarn A and bind off in rib.

FINISHING

Block to measurements. With RS together fold the two ends toward the center, using markers as top and bottom of pillow cover, and overlapping center back of pillow cover by 4in (10cm). Sew side seams. Turn RS out. Insert pillow form.

Seed-stitch Camisole

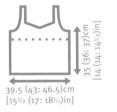

39.5 (43: 46.5)cm
[15½ (17: 18¼)in]

35 (36: 37)cm
[14 (14: 14½)in]

SIZES & YARNS

Size	S	M	L	
To fit bust	30-32	34	36	in
	76-81	86	91	cm
Actual size	31	34	36½	in
	79	86	93	cm
Center back length	14	14¼	14½	in
	35	36	37	cm

Rowan Cotton Glace, 50g balls

A Pale lime (813)	6	6	7
B Lavender (787)	1	1	1

2yd (1.8m) narrow maroon ribbon

NEEDLES

1 pair size 2 (2.75mm) needles and size 3 (3.25mm) needles.

Size D/3 (3mm) crochet hook.

1 stitch holder.

GAUGE

24 sts and 34 rows to 4in (10cm) measured over seed st using size 3 (3.25mm) needles.

BACK

Using size 2 (2.75mm) needles and yarn A, cast on 95 (103: 111) sts.

Work 6 rows in K1, P1 rib.

Change to size 3 (3.25mm) needles and work in 3 x 1 rib as folls:

Row 1 (RS) *K3, P1, rep from * to last 3 sts, K3.

Row 2 *P3, K1, rep from * to last 3 sts, P3.

Rep rows 1 and 2 until work meas 8½in (21cm), ending with row 1.

Make eyelets

Next row (WS) *P2tog, yo, P1, K1, rep from * to last 3 sts, P2tog, yo, P1.

Work 2 rows more in rib.

Change to seed st and cont until work meas 14 (14¼: 14½)in [35 (36: 37)cm], ending ready for a RS row.

Shape armholes

Rows 1 and 2 Bind off 5 (6: 7) sts at beg of row.

Dec 1 st at each end of next 6 (8: 10) rows. 73 (75: 77) sts.

Divide for neck

Next row Seed st 36 (37: 38), and put on holder, bind off 1 st, seed st to end. 36 (37: 38) sts.

Row 1 Dec 1 st at each end of row.

Row 2 Dec 1 st at neck edge.

Rep rows 1 and 2 until 6 (5: 5) sts rem. Size 1 only, dec 1 st at neck edge on next row.

Cont on these 5 sts until seed st section of work meas 11in (28cm). Bind off.

With WS facing, rejoin yarn to rem sts at center and work to match first side, reversing shaping.

FRONT

Make a second piece to match.

FINISHING

Block to measurements. Sew shoulder and side seams.

Picot edging With RS facing and yarn B, work one round of picot edging around armholes and neck as folls: *Work 3sc along edge, then ch3 and join with a slip st to last sc to make picot, rep from *.

Weave in any loose ends.

Weave ribbon through eyelets and tie at front.

Laundry Bag

SIZE & YARNS

Size   20 x 24in

                51.5 x 61cm

Rowan 4ply Cotton, 50g balls

A White (113)	7
B Lavender (127)	1

NEEDLES

Size 3 (3mm) circular needle at least 24in (61cm) long.

Size D/3 (3mm) crochet hook.

GAUGE

28 sts and 38 rows to 4in (10cm) measured over pattern using size 3 (3mm) needles.

BAG

Using size 3 (3mm) needles and yarn A, cast on 144 sts and work back and forth for 2½in (6cm) in St st.

Make eyelets

Row 1 K4, *yo, K2tog, K5, rep from * to last 3 sts, end yo, K2tog, K1.

Row 2 Purl.

Work 2 rows in St st.

Change to diamond patt as folls:

Row 1 *P1, K7, rep from * to end.

Row 2 *K1, P5, K1, P1, rep from * to end.

Row 3 *K2, P1, K3, P1, K1, rep from * to end.

Row 4 *P2, K1, P1, K1, P3, rep from * to end.

Row 5 *K4, P1, K3, rep from * to end.

Row 6 Rep row 4.

Row 7 Rep row 3.

Row 8 Rep row 2.

Rows 1 to 8 form diamond patt rep.

Rep rows 1 to 8 until work meas approx 24in (61cm), ending with a WS row.

Bind off.

Make second piece to match.

FINISHING

Weave in any loose ends. Block to measurements. Place RS together, taking care to match diamonds and eyelets, and sew side and bottom seams.

Using size D/3 (3mm) crochet hook and yarn B, work a picot edging around top opening of bag as folls:

Work a round of single crochet around top.

Next round *1sc in each of next 3sc, then ch3 and join with a slip st to last sc to make picot, rep from * to end.

Make 2 drawstring ties by using 3 strands of yarn B and working a crochet chain for 50in (127cm), leaving 3in (7cm) lengths at each end for tassels. Thread through eyelets, one each way (see photograph), and pull to close bag.

Wash Bag

SIZE & YARNS

Size   10 x 13in
              25 x 33cm

Rowan 4ply Cotton, 50g balls

A Lavender (127)	2
B Pale lime (134)	1

NEEDLES

1 pair of size 3 (3mm) needles.
Size D/3 (3mm) crochet hook.

GAUGE

28 sts and 38 rows to 4in (10cm) measured over pattern using size 3 (3mm) needles.

BAG

Using size 3 (3mm) needles and yarn A, cast on 72 sts and work 2in (5cm) in St st.

Make eyelets

Row 1 K4, *yo, K2tog, K5, rep from * to last 3 sts, end yo, K2tog, K1.

Row 2 Purl.

Work 2 rows n St st.Change to diamond patt as folls:

Row 1 *P1, K7, rep from * to end.

Row 2 *K1, P5, K1, P1, rep from * to end

Row 3 *K2, P1, K3, P1, K1, rep from * to end.

Row 4 *P2, K1, P1, K1, P3, rep from * to end.

Row 5 *K4, P1, K3, rep from * to end.

Row 6 Rep row 4.

Row 7 Rep row 3.

Row 8 Rep row 2.

Rows 1 to 8 form diamond patt rep.

Rep rows 1 to 8 until work meas approx 13in (33cm), ending with a WS row.

Bind off.

Make second piece to match.

FINISHING

Weave in any loose ends.Block pieces to measurements. Place RS together, taking care to match diamonds and eyelets, and sew side and bottom seams.

Using size D/3 (3mm) crochet hook and yarn B, work a picot edging around top opening of bag as folls:

Work a round of single crochet around top.

Next round *1sc in each of next 3sc, then ch3 and join with a slip st to last sc to make picot, rep from * to end.

Make 2 drawstring ties by using 3 strands of yarn B and working a crochet chain for 30in (76cm), leaving 3in (7cm) lengths at each end for tassels. Thread through eyelets, one each way, and pull to close bag.

USEFUL INFORMATION

Knitting Techniques

Included here is information that will help you follow knitting patterns and achieve success with your knits. (See page 117 for knitting abbreviations.)

GAUGE

Obtaining the correct gauge (the correct number of stitches and rows per in/cm) is perhaps the single factor that can make the difference between a successful piece of knitting and a disastrous one. It is especially important for knitted garments. Gauge controls both the shape and size of an article, so any variation, however slight, can distort the finished garment. We recommend that you begin by casting on 5 to 10 stitches more than specified for 4 inches in the gauge information section and work the pattern stitch indicated for 5 to 10 rows more than necessary for 4 inches. Bind off, wash the swatch, pat it out and let it dry thoroughly. Place pins at the edges of the specified number of stitches and rows, then measure to see whether the space between the pins equals 4 inches. If the square is smaller than 4 inches, go up in needle size; if it is larger, go down in needle size. Note: it is generally more important that you achieve the correct stitch gauge than the correct row gauge. Once you have achieved the correct gauge, you can be certain that your garment will be knit to the measurements indicated.

SIZES

In a pattern that is written for more than one size, the first number given is for the smallest size and the numbers for the larger sizes are inside the parentheses. When there is only one number, this applies to all sizes. Be sure to follow the stitch counts and measurements for your chosen size throughout. When choosing which size to knit, look first at the actual measurement around the garment at the underarm point—this is given under the size list at the beginning of the pattern. A useful tip is to measure one of your own garments that fits you comfortably. Having chosen an appropriate pattern size based on width, look at the corresponding length for that size; if you are not happy with the recommended length, adjust your own garment before beginning your armhole shaping—any adjustment after this point will prevent your sleevecap from fitting into the armholes properly. Don't forget to take your adjustment into account if there is any side shaping.

Measure your body between the center of your neck and your wrist; this measurement should correspond to half the garment width plus the sleeve length. Again, your sleeve length may be adjusted, but remember to take into consideration your sleeve increases if you do adjust the length—you must increase more frequently than the pattern states to shorten your sleeve, less frequently to lengthen it.

KNITTING WITH COLOR

There are two main methods of working color into a knitted fabric—the intarsia and Fair Isle techniques. The first method produces a single thickness of fabric and is usually used where a color is only required in a particular area of a row and does not form a repeating pattern across the row, as in the Fair Isle technique.

INTARSIA The simplest way to work the intarsia technique is to cut short lengths of yarn for each motif or block of color used in a row. To avoid gaps when changing from one color to another in a row, always bring the new color yarn **over** the yarn you have just used. Do not twist the yarns together. All loose ends can either be darned in later along the color join lines, or can be woven into the back of the knitting as each color is used. Weaving in the ends while knitting is done in much the same way as weaving in yarns when working the Fair Isle technique and does save time darning-in ends later.

FAIR ISLE TYPE KNITTING When two or three colors are worked repeatedly across a row, strand the yarn not in use loosely across the wrong side of the knitting. If you are working with more than two colors, treat the floating yarns as if they were one yarn and always spread the stitches to their correct width to keep them elastic. It is advisable not to carry the stranded or floating yarns over more than one inch at a time, but to weave them under and over the color you are working, catching them into the back of the work. It is essential that the gauge be noted for Fair Isle because it will be denser than one-color St st gauge.

FINISHING INSTRUCTIONS

The pieces for your knitted garment or other projects may take hours to complete, so it would be a great pity to spoil the work by taking too little care in the blocking and finishing process. Follow these tips for professional-looking knits.

BLOCKING Spread out each piece of knitting to the correct measurements and pin it to a backing cloth—this is called "blocking." Following the instructions on the yarn label, steam or spritz the pieces, taking care not to press on the surface of the knitting with a hot iron. Take special care to make the edges neat, as this will make seaming easier. Allow to dry thoroughly. Darn in all ends neatly along the selvage edge or a color join, as appropriate.

SEWING SEAMS When sewing knitted pieces together, remember to match areas of color and texture very carefully where they meet. Use a seam stitch such as backstitch or mattress stitch (an edge-to-edge stitch) for all main knitting seams. Join all ribbing (and neckbands) with mattress stitch, unless otherwise stated.

JOINING GARMENT PIECES When sewing the seams on a knitted garment, start by joining the left shoulder and neckband seams as explained above.

Then sew the top of the sleeve to the body of the garment using the method recommended in the pattern. The following are the techniques for different sleeve types:

Straight bound-off sleeves: Aligning the center of the bound-off edge of the sleeve with the shoulder seam, sew the top of the sleeve to the body, using markers as guidelines where applicable.

Square set-in sleeves: Aligning the center of the bound-off edge of the sleeve with the shoulder seam, set the sleeve cap into the armhole so that the straight sides at the top of the sleeve form a neat right-angle with the armhole bound-off stitches on the back and front.

Shallow set-in sleeves: Aligning the center of the bound-off edge of the sleeve with the shoulder seam, join the bound-off stitches at the beginning of the armhole shaping with the bound-off stitches at the start of the sleeve cap shaping. Sew the sleeve cap into the armhole, easing in the shapings.

Set-in sleeves: Aligning the center of the bound-off edge of the sleeve with the shoulder seam, set in the sleeve, easing the sleeve cap into the armhole.

After joining the top of the sleeves to the back and front of the garment, join the side and sleeve seams.

Next, slip stitch any pocket edgings and linings in place, sew on button bands (if necessary) and sew on buttons to correspond with buttonholes.

Lastly, press seams, avoiding ribbing and any areas of garter stitch.

Abbreviations

These are the general knitting abbreviations used in this book.

alt	alternate
beg	begin(ning)
cm	centimeter(s)
cont	continu(e)(ing)
dec	decreas(e)(ing)
foll(s)	follow(s)(ing)
garter st	garter stitch (K every row)
in	inch(es)
inc	increase(e)(ing); in a row instruction, work into front and back of stitch
K	knit
m	meter(s)
M1	make one stitch by picking up horizontal loop before next stitch and knitting into back of it
M1P	make one stitch by picking up horizontal loop before next stitch and purling into back of it

meas	measures
mm	millimeter(s)
seed st	work in seed stitch (see right)
P	purl
patt	pattern; work in pattern
rem	remain(s)(ing)
rep	repeat(ing)
rev St st	reverse stockinette stitch (purl all RS rows, knit all WS rows)
RS	right side(s)
sl1	slip one stitch
ssk	slip the next 2 sts one at a time as if to knit, then knit them tog.
st(s)	stitch(es)
St st	stockinette stitch (K all RS rows, P all WS rows)
tbl	through back of loop(s)
tog	together
WS	wrong side(s)
yb	yarn to back of work between two needles
yd	yard(s)

yf	yarn to front of work between two needles
yo	yarn over right-hand needle to make a new stitch
o (zero)	no stitches, times or rows

SEED STITCH Where a pattern calls for seed st, work over even number of stitches as folls:
Seed st row 1 (K1, P1) to end.
Seed st row 2 (P1, K1) to end.
Rep rows 1 and 2 for patt.
Work over an odd number of stitches as folls.
Seed st row 1 *K1, P1, rep from * to last st, K1.
Rep row 1 for patt.

3-NEEDLE BIND-OFF Place RS tog, back sts on one needle and front sts on another. Using 3rd needle, *K 2 sts tog (1 from front needle, 1 from back needle). Rep from * once. Pass first st over 2nd st. [1st bound off]. Cont to knit 2 tog (1 front st and 1 back st) and bind off across.

Yarn Information

The following list covers the Rowan yarns used in this book. All the information was correct at the time of publication, but yarn companies change their products frequently and cannot absolutely guarantee that the shades or yarn types used will be available when you come to use these patterns. The yarn descriptions here will help you find a substitute if necessary. If substituting yarn, always remember to calculate the yarn amount needed by metrage/yardage rather than by ball weight.

Note: Always check the yarn label for care instructions.

Rowan Cotton Glace
A medium-weight cotton yarn; 100 percent cotton
Ball size 50g/1 ¾ oz ball; about 126yds (115m)
Recommended gauge 23 sts and 32 rows to 4in (10cm) measured over St st using sizes 3–5 (3.25–3.75mm) needles

Rowan 4ply Cotton
A lightweight cotton yarn; 100 percent cotton
Ball size 50g/1¾oz; about 186yds (170m)
Recommended gauge 27–29 sts and 37–39 rows to 4in (10cm) measured over St st using sizes 2–3 (3–3.25mm) needles

Rowan 4ply Soft
A lightweight wool yarn; 100 percent merino wool
Ball size 50g/1¾oz; about 191yds (175m)
Recommended gauge 28 sts and 36 rows to 4in (10cm) measured over St st using size 3 (3.25mm) needles

Rowan Handknit DK Cotton
A medium-weight cotton yarn; 100 percent cotton
Ball size 50g/1¾oz; about 93yds (85m)
Recommended gauge 19–20 sts and 28 rows to 4in (10cm) measured over St st using sizes 6–7 (4–4.5mm) needles

Rowan Kid Classic
A medium-weight mohair-mix yarn; 70 percent lambswool, 26 percent kid mohair, 4 percent nylon
Ball size 50g/1¾oz; about 153yds (140m)
Recommended gauge 18–19 sts and 23–25 rows to 4in (10cm) measured over St st using sizes 8–9 (5–5.5mm) needles

Rowan Kidsilk Haze
A lightweight mohair-mix yarn; 70 percent super kid mohair, 30 percent silk
Ball size 25g/1oz; about 229yds (210m)
Recommended gauge 18–25 sts and 23–34 rows to 4in (10cm) measured over St st using sizes 3–8 (3.25–5mm) needles

Rowan Polar
A chunky wool-mix yarn; 60 percent pure new wool, 30 percent alpaca, 10 percent acrylic
Ball size 100g/3½oz; about 109yds (100m)
Recommended gauge 12 sts and 16 rows to 4in (10cm) measured over St st using size 11 (8mm) needles

Rowan Summer Tweed
A medium-weight silk/cotton blend yarn; 70 percent silk, 30 percent cotton
Hank size 50g/1¾oz; about 118yds (108m)
Recommended gauge 16 sts and 23 rows to 4in (10cm) measured over St st using size 8 (5mm) needles

Rowan Wool Cotton
A medium-weight wool/cotton blend yarn; 50 percent merino wool, 50 percent cotton
Ball size 50g/1¾oz; about 123yds (113m)
Recommended gauge 22–24 sts and 30–32 rows to 4in (10cm) measured over St st using sizes 5–6 (3.75–4mm) needles

Rowan Yorkshire Tweed DK
A medium-weight wool yarn; 100 percent pure new wool
Ball size 50g/1¾oz; about 123yds (113m)
Recommended gauge 20–22 sts and 28–30 rows to 4in (10cm) measured over St st using size 6 (4mm) needles

Rowan Yorkshire Tweed 4ply
A lightweight wool yarn; 100 percent pure new wool
Ball size 25g/1oz; about 120yds (110m)
Recommended gauge 26–28 sts and 38–40 rows to 4in (10cm) measured over St st using sizes 2–3 (3–3.25mm) needles

Buying Yarn

For the best results, always use the yarn specified in your knitting pattern. Use the addresses below to find your nearest supplier.

ROWAN YARN ADDRESSES

U.S.A. Rowan USA, c/o Westminster Fibers Inc., 4 Townsend West, Suite 8, Nashua, NH 03063. Tel: +1 (603) 886 5041/5043. E-mail: rowan@westminsterfibers.com

U.K. Rowan, Green Lane Mill, Holmfirth, West Yorkshire HD9 2DX, England. Tel: +44 (o) 1484 681 881. Fax: +44 (o) 1484 687 920. www.knitrowan.com

Australia Australian Country Spinners, 314 Albert Street, Brunswick, Victoria 3056. Tel: (03) 9380 3888.

Belgium Pavan, Meerlaanstraat 73, B9860 Balegem (Oosterzele). Tel: (32) 9 221 8594. E-mail: pavan@pandora.be

Canada Diamond Yarn, 9697 St Laurent, Montreal, Quebec, H3L 2N1. Tel: (514) 388 6188. Diamond Yarn (Toronto), 155 Martin Ross, Unit 3, Toronto, Ontario M3J 2L9. Tel: (416) 736 6111. www.diamondyarns.com E-mail: diamond@diamondyarn.com

Denmark Designvaerkstedet, Boulevarden 9, Aalborg 9000. Tel: (45) 9812 0713. Fax: (45) 9813 0213. Inger's, Volden 19, Aarhus 8000. Tel: (45) 8619 4044. Sommerfuglen, Vandkunsten 3, Kobenhaven K 1467. Tel: (45) 3332 8290. E-mail: mail@sommerfuglen.dk www.sommerfuglen.dk Uldstedet, Fiolstraede 13, Kobehavn K 1171. Tel/Fax: (45) 3391 1771. Uldstedet, G1. Jernbanevej 7, Lyngby 2800. Tel/Fax: (45) 4588 1088. Garnhoekeren, Karen Olsdatterstraede 9, Roskilde 4000. Tel/Fax: (45) 4637 2063.

France Elle Tricot, 8 Rue du Coq, 67000 Strasbourg. Tel: (33) 3 88 23 03 13. E-mail: HYPERLINK "mailto:elletricot@agat.net" elletricot@agat.net.   www.elletricote.com
Germany Wolle & Design, Wolfshovener Strasse 76, 52428 Julich-Stetternich. Tel: (49) 2461 54735. www.wolleunddesign.de E-mail: Info@wolleunddesign.de

Holland de Afstap, Oude Leliestraat 12, 1015 AW Amsterdam. Tel: (31) 20 6231445.

Hong Kong East Unity Co. Ltd., Unit B2, 7/F Block B, Kailey Industrial Centre, 12 Fung Yip Street, Chai Wan. Tel: (852) 2869 7110. Fax (852) 2537 6952. E-mail: eastuni@netvigator.com

Iceland Storkurinn, Laugavegi 59, 101 Reykjavik. Tel: (354) 551 8258. Fax: (354) 562 8252. E-mail: malin@mmedia.is

Japan Puppy Co. Ltd., T151-0051, 3-16-5 Sendagaya, Shibuyaku, Tokyo. Tel: (81) 3 3490 2827. E-mail: info@rowan-jaeger.com

Korea De Win Co. Ltd., Chongam Bldg, 101, 34-7 Samsung-dong, Seoul. Tel: (82) 2 511 1087. E-mail: knittking@yahoo.co.kr

www.dewin.co.kr My Knit Studio, (3F) 121 Kwan Hoon Dong, Chongro-ku, Seoul. Tel: (82) 2 722 0006. E-mail: myknit@myknit.com

New Zealand Alterknitives, P.O. Box 47961, Ponsonby, Auckland. Tel: (64) 9 376 0337. E-mail: knitit@ihug.co.nz Knit World, P.O. Box 30 645, Lower Hutt. Tel: (64) 4 586 4530. E-mail: knitting@xtra.co.nz The Stitchery, Shop 8, Suncourt Shopping Centre, 1111 Taupo. Tel: (64) 7 378 9195.

Norway Paa Pinne, Tennisvn 3D, 0777 Oslo. Tel: (47) 909 62 818.   www.paapinne.no E-mail: design@paapinne.no

Spain Oyambre, Pau Claris 145, 80009 Barcelona. Tel: (34) 670 011957. E-mail : comercial@oyambreonline.com

Sweden Wincent, Norrtullsgatan 65, 113 45 Stockholm. Tel: (46) 8 33 70 60. E-mail: wincent@chello.se www.wincent.nu

Acknowledgments

Author's Acknowledgments

My warmest thanks to all the people who have
contributed to this book for their enthusiasm,
encouragement, and commitment.
Stephen Sheard, Kate Buller, Ann Hinchcliffe
and Sarah Hatton at Rowan; Eva Yates,
Gill Everett and her team of knitters;
Stella Smith; Sally Harding, Hilary Laurence,
and Elizabeth Dallas; Chloe, Josie, Hannah
and Alicia; Catherine Gratwicke, Francine Kay
and Alesse Bowditch, Georgina Rhodes, and
Susan Berry.
To Georgina Dallas who inspired the idea for
the book.
And especially to my family for their constant
support and endless patience.

Publisher's Acknowledgments

The publishers would like to thank everyone
on the team who helped to put this book
together, in particular Georgina Rhodes
and Richard Proctor, Catherine Gratwicke,
Francine Kay, Eva Yates, Stella Smith,
and Sally Harding.